THE MATRIX

A LOOK

INSIDE

DOMESTIC VIOLENCE

R. Vanessa Whiting

I dedicate this book to my friends who are still experiencing domestic violence and abuse. I pray that they will receive the help that they need; so they can experience the victory that I have, now that I am a survivor and free

Table of Contents

∞

Acknowledgement

∞

During the course of this project; many people provided support, guidance, assistance and prayer. Special acknowledgements are extended to the following individuals to whom I will always be grateful.

Many thanks, to Dr. Lalita Maz; for her continued support, patience and encouragement. Thanks to, Pastor, Michael Macauley for his dedication to ministry, his prayers and the observance of the call that God has placed on my life, along with the gentle nudging that he gives to ensure I fulfill that calling, to Daniel Kuetemeyer for his patience with me and kindness throughout the design process on this project, special thanks to Larry Walker Jr. for his support, affirming words and reminder to believe in myself while looking to God for strength because all things are possible with Him. Also; want to thank my family and friends who were a part of encouraging, praying and walking along side of me throughout this process.

Great thanks to my children Billy Jr. aka B.J and Marquita Newton; who have endured this journey with me and are working through their own traumatic experiences but was still able to encourage, support and help drive me to continue the pursuit of my dream which is to help others. I love you both dearly, admire your strength and so very proud of who you are becoming. Keep pressing forward; the best is yet to come.

Preface

∞

As a survivor of Domestic Violence; I was not aware of the early signs of abuse nor did I have any options, resources or places to turn while going through my journey. I saw the importance of providing a source of information that could get the hard conversation started. Silence hides violence. Where do we go from here?!...let's start talking.

This book was written out of a heart of compassion for helping others in a Domestic Violence situation or for anyone who knows someone that may be suffering in silence and believe there is no way out. It is designed to educate on the causes, consequences and traumatic effects of the abuse.

The goal is to be a guide to victims; a source of reference to help recognize the subtle or even more obvious signs and symptoms of abuse.

Enlighten family members of victims, support systems and society as a whole; so we can come to understand what is happening right around us.

Introduction

∞

Surviving domestic violence and having the courage to speak about it, is a victory. Having previously been married for fifteen years to a "Christian man"; who everyone around me thought was the ideal husband, father and man after God's own heart, was very disappointed to find out that he was an abusive man. His level of abuse wasn't limited to one type; it was emotional, verbal and ultimately physical.

As an abuser he knew how to conduct himself in the presence of others but behind closed doors he was a different person. He became at times like a Dr. Jekyll/ Mr. Hyde; I have to believe we all know the story of those two. It was not easy living with someone that could be very sweet in one moment and turn on you with little warning.

The problem with the Christian abuser is that pastors, lay pastors and even Christian counselors are not usually fully equipped to deal with such a difficult situation in the family of faith. So because of this; the victim, who is usually a woman, would go to her leaders in the church and express her concerns about her husband's current behavior that is causing her to become fearful of him, to be told that "Christ suffered therefore sometimes in life we have to suffer".

When dealing with a woman who feels abused and is reaching out for help; that is not the answer she expects to hear. When receiving an answer such as that, the Christian woman tends to struggle going forward with whether or not she was doing the right thing in seeking counsel.

In turn, she would keep quiet; suffer in silence with her abuser and experience continued abuse and in extreme cases, death.

During a night of rage; my ex-husband/abuser placed a nine millimeter semi-automatic handgun at my temple with the intent to kill but the trigger didn't engage, not allowing the fatal bullet to escape the chamber and end my life, which in turn allows me to tell a part of my story. Being that I have been a victim and now a survivor, I understand that domestic violence is a topic that needs more discussion. Silence kills, let's start talking!

1

What is Domestic Violence?

∞

Domestic violence is the willful intimidation, physical assault, battery, sexual assault, and/or other abusive behavior as part of a systematic pattern of power and control perpetrated by one intimate partner against another. It includes physical violence, sexual violence and psychological violence, verbal and emotional abuse.

The frequency and severity of domestic violence can vary dramatically; however, the one constant component of domestic violence is one partner's consistent efforts to maintain power and control over the other.

Domestic violence is an epidemic affecting individuals in every community, regardless of age, economic status, sexual orientation, gender, race, religion, or nationality. It is often accompanied by emotionally abusive and controlling behavior that is only a fraction of a systematic pattern of dominance and control.

3

Domestic violence can result in physical injury, psychological trauma, and in severe cases, even death. The devastating physical, emotional, and psychological consequences of domestic violence can cross generations and last a lifetime. It is not always easy to determine in the early stages of a relationship if one person will become abusive.

Domestic violence intensifies over time. Abusers may often seem wonderful and perfect initially, but gradually become more aggressive and controlling as the relationship continues. Abuse may begin with behaviors that may easily be dismissed or downplayed such as name calling, threats, possessiveness, or distrust. Abusers may apologize profusely for their actions or try to convince the person they are abusing that they do these things out of love or care. However, violence and control always intensifies over time with an abuser, despite the apologies. What may start out as something that was first believed to be harmless (e.g., wanting the victim to spend all their time only with them because they love them so much) escalates into extreme control and abuse (e.g., threatening to kill or hurt the victim or others if they speak to family, friends, etc.). Some examples of abusive tendencies include but are not limited to just one:

- Telling the victim that they can never do anything right

- Showing jealousy of the victim's family and friends and time spent away

- Accusing the victim of cheating

- Keeping or discouraging the victim from seeing friends or family members

- Embarrassing or shaming the victim with put-downs

- Controlling every penny spent in the household

- Taking the victim's money or refusing to give them money for expenses

- Looking at or acting in ways that scare the person they are abusing

- Controlling who the victim sees, where they go, or what they do

- Dictating how the victim dresses, wears their hair, etc.

- Stalking the victim or monitoring their victim's every move (in person or also via the internet and/or other devices such as GPS tracking or the victim's phone)

- Preventing the victim from making their own decisions

- Telling the victim that they are a bad parent or threatening to hurt, kill, or take away their children

- Threatening to hurt or kill the victim's friends, loved ones, or pets

- Intimidating the victim with guns, knives, or other weapons

- Pressuring the victim to have sex when they don't want to or to do things sexually they are not comfortable with
- Forcing sex with others
- Refusing to use protection when having sex or sabotaging birth control
- Pressuring or forcing the victim to use drugs or alcohol
- Preventing the victim from working or attending school, harassing the victim at either work or school, keeping their victim up all night so they perform badly at their job or in school
- Destroying the victim's property

It is important to note that domestic violence does not always manifest as physical abuse. Emotional and psychological abuse can often be just as extreme as physical violence. Lack of physical violence does not mean the abuser is any less dangerous to the victim nor does it mean the victim is any less trapped by the abuse.

Additionally, domestic violence does not always end when the victim escapes the abuser, tries to terminate the relationship, and /or seeks help. Often, it intensifies because the abuser feels a loss of control over the victim. Abusers frequently continue to stalk, harass, threaten, and try to control the victim after the victim escapes. In fact, the victim is often in the most danger directly following the escape of the relationship or when they seek help. One fifth of homicide victims with restraining orders are murdered within two days of obtaining the order; One third is murdered within the first month.

Unfair blame is frequently put upon the victim of abuse because of assumptions that victims choose to stay in abusive relationships. The truth is, bringing an end to abuse is not a matter of the victim choosing to leave; it is a matter of the victim being able to safely *escape* their abuser, the abuser choosing to stop the abuse, or others (e.g., law enforcement, courts) holding the abuser accountable for the abuse they inflict.

2

Dynamics of Abuse

∞

Anyone can be a victim of domestic violence. There is NO "typical victim." Victims of domestic violence come from all walks of life, varying age groups, All backgrounds, All communities, All education levels, All economic levels, All cultures, All ethnicities, All religions, All abilities, and All lifestyles.

Victims of domestic violence do not bring violence upon themselves, they do not always lack self-confidence, nor are they just as abusive as the abuser. Violence in relationships occurs when one person feels entitled to power and control over their partner and chooses to use abuse to gain and maintain that control.

In relationships where domestic violence exists, violence is not equal, even if the victim fights back or instigates violence in an effort to diffuse a situation. There is always one person who is the primary, constant source of power, control, and abuse in the relationship.

Every relationship differs, but what is most common within all abusive relationships is the varying tactics used by abusers to gain and maintain power and control over the victim. Nearly 3 in 10 women and 1 in 10 men in the United States have experienced rape, physical violence, and/or stalking by an intimate partner [or former partner] and reported at least one impactful related experience or other forms of violent behavior in the relationship (i.e., feeling fearful, concern for safety, post-traumatic stress disorder (PTSD), need for health care, injury, crisis support, for housing services, victim advocacy services, legal services, missed work or school).

Physical and sexual assaults, or threats to commit them, are the most apparent forms of domestic violence and are usually the actions that make others aware of the problem. However; regular use of other abusive behaviors by the abuser, when reinforced by one or more acts of physical violence, make up a larger scope of abuse. Although physical assaults may occur only occasionally, they instill fear of future violent attacks and allow the abuser to control the victim's life and circumstances.

Very often, one or more violent incidents are accompanied by an array of these other types of abuse; sexual, emotional, economic and psychological. They are less easily identified, yet firmly establish a pattern of intimidation and control in the relationship. There are periods of time where things may be calmer, but those times are followed by a buildup of tension and abuse, which usually results in the abuser peaking with intensified abuse.

The cycle then often starts to repeat, commonly becoming more and more intense as time goes on. Each relationship is different and not every relationship follows the exact pattern. Some abusers may cycle rapidly, others over longer stretches of time. Regardless, abusers purposefully use numerous tactics of abuse to instill fear in the victim and maintain control over them.

Domestic violence affects all aspects of a victim's life. When abuse victims are able to safely escape and remain free from their abuser, they often survive with long-lasting and sometimes permanent effects to their mental and physical health; relationships with friends, family, and children; their career; and their economic well-being.

Victims of domestic violence experience an array of emotions and feelings from the abuse inflicted upon them by their abuser, both within and

11

following the relationship. They may also resort to extremes, in effort to cope with the abuse. Victims of domestic violence may:

- Want the abuse to end, but not the relationship

- Feel isolated

- Feel depressed

- Feel helpless

- Be unaware of what services are available to help them

- Be embarrassed of their situation

- Fear judgment or stigmatization if they reveal the abuse

- Deny or minimize the abuse or make excuses for the abuser

- Still love their abuser

- Withdraw emotionally

- Distance themselves from family or friends

- Be impulsive or aggressive

- Feel financially dependent on their abuser

- Feel guilt related to the relationship

- Feel shame

- Have anxiety

- Have suicidal thoughts

- Abuse alcohol or drugs

- Be hopeful that their abuser will change and /or stop the abuse

- Have religious, cultural, or other beliefs that reinforce staying in the relationship

- Have no support from friends of family

- Fear cultural, community, or societal backlash that may hinder escape or support

- Feel like they have nowhere to go or no ability to get away

- Fear they will not be able to support themselves after they escape the abuser

- Have children in common with their abuser and fear for their safety if they leave

- Have pets or other animals they don't want to leave

- Be distrustful of local law enforcement, courts, or other systems if the abuse is revealed

- Have had unsupportive experiences with friends, family, employers, law enforcement, courts, child protective services, etc. and either believe they won't get help if they leave or fear retribution if they do (e.g., they fear they will lose custody of their children to the abuser)

These are among the many reasons victims of domestic violence either choose to stay in abusive relationship or feel they are unable to leave.

The idea that individuals would use physical violence against those they are supposed to love seems both contradictory and unlikely. Yet it is becoming increasingly clear that individuals do use violence within their intimate relationships. In addition, the number of families and couples affected by violence is far more extensive than we can ever imagine.

3

Characteristics of an Abuser

∞

Anyone can be an abuser. They come from all groups, all cultures, all religions, all economic levels, and all backgrounds. They can be your neighbor, your pastor, your friend, your child's teacher, a relative, a coworker or anyone. It is important to note that the majority of abusers are only violent with their current or past intimate partners. One study found that 90% of abusers do not have criminal records and that abusers are generally law-abiding outside of the home. There is no one, typical, detectable personality of an abuser. However, they do often display common characteristics.

- An abuser often denies the existence or minimizes the seriousness of the violence and its effect on the victim and other family members.
- An abuser objectifies the victim and often sees them as their property or sexual objects.

- An abuser has low self-esteem and feels powerless and ineffective in the world. He or she may appear successful, but internally, they feel inadequate.

- An abuser externalizes the causes of their behavior. They blame their violence on circumstances such as stress, their partner's behavior, a "bad day," on alcohol, drugs, or other factors.

- An abuser may be pleasant and charming between periods of violence and is often seen as a "nice person" to others outside of the relationship.

- An abuser may use coercion, intimidation, threats, isolation, emotional abuse, economic abuse, and/ or the children to control the partner.

Red flags and warning signs of an abuser include but are not limited to:

- Extreme jealousy

Some believe that jealous feelings are normal as long as they are not attached to intimidation, isolation or stalking. That would seem to be a reasonable position toward occasional feelings in a non-oppressive relationship. However, constant looming jealously and un-justified suspicions with anger attachment does quite the damage to a victim.

The walking on egg shells; causes a victim to limit and distort normal social interaction. Jealousy can lead to severe aggression that causes suspicions of infidelity and that aggression can be used to force the victim into confessions of infidelity which the abuser will then use to justify the abuse.

- Possessiveness

A relationship can become suffocating when one wants to control the other in every possible way: where you go, who you talk to, what you do etc. We should understand that people don't belong to us; each individual has a right to their own freedom. Possessiveness often times leads to jealousy, a contributor to abuse. Signs of possession in a relationship include disallowing your significant other from seeing his / or her friends and family, getting upset if they speak to the opposite sex, frequently checking up on them to name a few more common signs.

- Unpredictability

The abuser is unpredictable in his mood and actions as any other person. When he realizes that you are unable to read his mind, then you are not who he thought you were. He gets scared because if you are not who he thought you were, then he can't control you. If he can't control you, his world shatters. The abuser gets upset when there is any trace of evidence showing that the victim is not doing, being or thinking like he does. The evidence that you are a separate person/ your own person with your own ideas or views, they tremble and lash out in a variety of methods to regain control of the victim.

- A bad temper

The public perceive domestic violence as one person losing their temper and striking another; do not be deceived. The demon we know as domestic violence would like for you to believe just that. The truth is; it is a matter of power and control. We all have tempers, to some extent, so can some control their temper more easily? Because it is a matter of power and control, not temper tantrums; when the abuser begins to think he is losing his prized possession, the cycle of fear, intimidation, isolation, the abuse is underway.

18

- Cruelty to animals

Abusers of animals are five times more likely to abuse a person. Nearly half of the victims who remain in violent households do so because they are afraid for their animals. Staying with an abuser puts every human and non-human at risk. Children in violent households, who have likely been abused themselves, represent one-fifth of domestic animal cruelty cases.

- Verbal abuse

Verbal abuse precedes the physical violence. This type attacks one's spirit and sense of self-worth. This type is not usually recognized as easily. It is a form of the power and control of the mind. Verbal abuse so controls one's mind that some women who have left a verbal abusive relationship twenty or even more years ago find themselves wondering if it was really abuse.

- Extremely controlling behavior

The idea of a man managing his wife and controlling his wife with absolute authority made its way into European society and law. For many centuries, including the Dark and Middle Ages as well as the

19

Renaissance, women were routinely subjugated. The physical punishment that accompanied their inferior status was justified by so-called "laws of chastisement". Although today we would label this behavior abusive.

- Antiquated beliefs about roles of women and men in relationships

- Forced sex or disregard of their partner's unwillingness to have sex

- Sabotage of birth control methods or refusal to honor agreed upon methods

- Blaming the victim for anything bad that happens

- Sabotage or obstruction of the victim's ability to work or attend school

- Their control of all finances

- Abuse of other family members, children, or pets

- Accusations of the victim flirting with others or having an affair

- Control of what the victim wears and how they act

- Demeaning the victim either privately or publicly

- Embarrassment or humiliation of the victim in front of others

- Harassment of the victim at work

4

Profile of an Abuser

∞

It's not easy to identify an abusive person by his appearance. An abuser does not grow horns and look like a snorting bull just before he smacks you across the face or hurls an arsenal of verbal weapons at you.

Many abusers are very charming, well-dressed, cultured people who act one way in public and another way at home. It is wrong to characterize an abuser as someone who is a drug addict or an alcoholic because most abusers are not either of those. Researchers in the field of abuse have drawn a variety of profiles of abusive men after years of working closely with them. They identify eight groups of batterers:

1. Men who are unable to control their impulses, who change swiftly in a Dr. Jekyll/ Mr. Hyde pattern

2. Men who demands strict adherence to rules and, with no emotion, mete out punishment to those who break them

21

3. Men who are rebellious, hostile, dependent, and low in self-esteem

4. Men who are aggressive and antisocial.

5. Men who exhibit great and inexplicable mood swings.

6. Men who are outwardly pleasant, but unable to handle rejection, aggressive when they feel their wife or girlfriend has let them down.

7. Men who are excessively dependent, anxious, and depressed

8. Men who show only minor signs of the other seven characteristics and have no psychopathology.

It is believed that the majority of abusers do not act out of mental illness, but instead from the socially developed use of immature or neurotic defense mechanisms to satisfy or seek to satisfy the emotional needs that may have been unfulfilled in childhood." What are defense mechanisms? They are the ways people handle conflicts. One person may handle failure by blaming someone else or striking out in rage while another person may either, deny it or laugh it off. Most abusers use three defense mechanisms: repression, acting out, and projection

5

Identifying Emotional Abuse

∞

Emotional Abuse is a type of domestic violence that is classified as the verbal or emotional debasement directed at one partner in an intimate partner relationship; although this type of domestic violence can be the most difficult to define, it is nonetheless an extremely serious offense, typically resulting in devastation, pain, and injury sustained by the victim of emotional abuse.

In certain cases, brief mentions of emotional abuse may be the only available signs suggesting that emotional or psychological abuse of this nature is taking place; in contrast, other individuations of emotional abuse may present themselves through vast changes in personality, avoidance of subject matter, as well as excuses set forth with regard to shifts in behavior

However, due to the fact that emotional abuse is largely difficult in its identification, the victim is considered to be the primary gateway through which emotional abuse is explored and prevented.

Certain victims of abuse may not be aware of the emotional abuse foisted upon them; emotional or psychological abuse entails any non-physical behavior to which an individual is exposed that, results in duress, psychological damage, emotional trauma, or intimidation.

Despite the alarming rate of emotional abuse facilitated through domestic violence, almost half of domestic violence abuse cases are not reported; due to the fact that both psychological and emotional abuse is largely difficult to identify, the testimony by victims of emotional abuse serve as the primary facilitation of efforts undertaken in order to put a stop to victimization from domestic violence.

However, it is not uncommon for victims of emotional abuse to refrain from reporting their respective victimization as a result of a variety of negative emotions, including fear, guilt, or anger.

In many cases, victims of emotional abuse will undergo a rampant and noticeable change in their respective personality; this can be illustrated through the avoidance of social interaction, the refusal to allow friends or family member's entry into the residence which the abuser lives, as well as the fabrication of events within their respective daily undertakings.

In other cases, victims of emotional abuse may volunteer information in an indirect fashion, which include the passing mention of abuse sustained or threats received by the individual victim; in addition, the presentation of spurious excuses and validation expressed by a victim of mental abuse with regard to their abusive partner are not uncommon.

Emotional abuse is a covert form of domestic violence that many people aren't able to recognize. This form of abuse is used to control, degrade, humiliate and punish a spouse/partner. While emotional abuse differs from physical abuse, the end result is the same. A spouse/partner becomes fearful and begins to change their behaviors to keep their abuser happy. The happier their partner, the less domestic violence the victim has to suffer.

By the time a victim identifies the true problem they have begun to feel as if they are crazy. They will doubt themselves and their own sense of reality because emotional abuse is meant to cause the victim to question their every thought and behavior.

This usually results in the victim having low self-esteem. Emotional abuse is crippling. It robs a person of the ability to think rationally, have confidence in themselves and their autonomy.

If your partner's words or behavior have caused any of the following feelings, it is time to seek help:

- Isolation from others, you rarely see friends and family.

- Excessive dependence on him/her.

- You constantly think about saying or doing the right thing so that your spouse does not become upset.

- You live in the moment, unable to plan ahead because you fear your spouse's response to any plans or ideas you have. Any action you take is criticized unless it is one of compliance to his/her desires.

- You feel as if you don't have the energy it would take to fight back against their controlling behavior. You doubt your ability to stand-up and speak your own mind and express your own opinions.

- You feel a sense of depression and anxiety most of the time.

- You feel as if anything you do or say will be met with anger or dismissal. Your feelings and desires just don't seem to matter to your spouse.

Victims that suffer emotional abuse also experience (PTSD) Post Traumatic Stress Disorder. Emotional numbness and avoidance can occur as a way of coping. Emotional numbing symptoms are part of the avoidance cluster of PTSD symptoms. Emotional numbing symptoms generally refer to those symptoms that reflect difficulties in experiencing positive emotions. Many people with PTSD try to escape their emotions. They may try to avoid thoughts, feelings or conversations about the traumatic event and places or people that bring the event to mind. Avoidance also refers to difficulty remembering important parts of the traumatic event and feeling as though life has been cut short.

Avoidance refers to any action designed to prevent the occurrence of an emotion or to stop feeling an uncomfortable emotion, such as fear, sadness or shame. For example, a person may try to avoid an emotion through the use of substances or dissociation.

Moreover, people experiencing avoidance may have emotional numbing symptoms such as feeling distant from others, losing interest in activities they used to enjoy or having trouble experiencing positive feelings such as happiness or love.

The first symptom includes the avoidance of emotional experiences, which is common among people with PTSD. It has been found that people with PTSD often try to avoid or "push away" their emotions, both emotions about a traumatic experience and emotions in general. Studies have found

27

that people with PTSD may withhold expressing emotions. In addition, it has been found that the avoidance of emotions may make some PTSD symptoms worsen or even contribute to the development of PTSD symptoms after the experience of a traumatic event.

Why avoidance doesn't work

Emotional avoidance is often considered an unhealthy coping strategy. It may be effective in the short-term and provide some temporary relief. However, in the long run, the emotions people are trying to avoid may actually grow stronger. That is, unless dealt with, those emotions don't really go away.

It is important to recognize that we have emotions for a reason. Our emotions provide us with information about ourselves and the things going on around us. For example, the emotion of fear tells us that we may be in danger.

The emotion of sadness tells us that we may need some time to take care of ourselves or seek help from others. Given the important role they play in our lives, our emotions are there to be experienced and they want to be experienced.

Basically, your emotions may "fight back," so they can be experienced and listened to. If someone is determined to avoid his/ her emotions, they may then turn to more drastic and unhealthy ways of avoiding emotions, such as through substance use.

Avoiding our emotions also takes considerable effort, especially when those emotions are strong (as they often are in PTSD). As avoided emotions grow stronger, more and more effort is needed to keep them at bay. As a result, little energy may be left for the important things in your life, such as family and friends. In addition, using all your energy to avoid certain emotions may make it difficult to manage other experiences, such as frustration and irritation, making you more likely to be "on edge" and angry.

What can be done?

The most important thing to do is to reduce the extent to which you try to escape your emotions. Of course, this is a lot easier said than done. If you have been avoiding your emotions for a long time, it may be difficult to release them. Sometimes, when we let our emotions build up, they may escape all at once, like a dam breaking. This may lead to our emotions feeling out of control.

It is important to find ways to release your emotions. Therapy of all kinds can be very helpful in this regard. Creation Therapy, Cognitive behavioral and psychoanalytic/psychodynamic therapies gives the opportunity to express and understand your emotions, as well as examine the sources of those emotional responses.

In addition to examining emotions connected directly to the traumatic event, cognitive-behavioral approaches may address how certain thoughts or ways of evaluating a situation may be contributing to your emotions. Creation Therapy or Acceptance and Commitment Therapy (or ACT), a particular type of behavior therapy, focuses on breaking down avoidance and helping a person place his/her energy into living a meaningful life (and being willing to experience whatever emotions arise as a result). Psychoanalytic/psychodynamic approaches focus more on early childhood experiences and their influence on your emotions.

Whichever therapy you choose, getting help can provide you with a safe place to express and approach your emotions. Seeking social support from trusted loved ones can also provide a safe way to express your emotions. Writing about your feelings can also give you a safe and private way to release your deepest feelings.

If your emotions feel really unclear or unpredictable, self-monitoring may be a useful strategy. It can give you a sense of which situations bring out certain thoughts and feelings. If your emotions feel too strong, try distraction instead of avoidance. Distraction can be viewed as "temporary avoidance."

Do something to temporarily distract you from a strong emotion, such as reading a book, calling a friend, eating comforting food or taking a bath. This may give the emotion some time to decrease in strength, making it easier to cope with.

6

Understanding why Victims Stay

∞

When it is a viable option, it is best for victims to do what they can to escape their abusers. However, this is not the case in all situations. Abusers repeatedly go to extremes to prevent the victim from leaving. In fact, leaving an abuser is the most dangerous time for a victim of domestic violence. One study found in interviews with men who have killed their wives that either threats of separation by their partner or actual separations were most often the precipitating events that lead to the murder.

A victim's reasons for staying with their abusers are extremely complex and, in most cases, are based on the reality that their abuser will follow through with the threats they have used to keep them trapped: the abuser will hurt or kill them, they will hurt or kill the kids, they will win custody of the children, they will harm or kill pets or others, they will ruin their victim financially—the list goes on. The victim in violent relationships knows their abuser best and fully knows the extent to which they will go to make sure they have and can maintain control over the victim. The victim literally may not be able to safely escape or protect those they love. A recent study of intimate partner homicides found that 20% of homicide victims were not the domestic violence victims themselves, but family members, friends, neighbors, persons who intervened, law enforcement responders, or bystanders.

Additional barriers to escaping a violent relationship include but are not limited to:

- The fear that the abuser's actions will become more violent, and may become lethal if the victim attempts to leave

- Unsupportive friends and family

- Knowledge of the difficulties of single parenting and reduced financial circumstances

- The victim feeling that the relationship is a mix of good times, love, and hope along with the manipulation, intimidation and fear

- The victim's lack of knowledge of or access to safety and support

- Fear of losing custody of any children if they leave or divorce their abuser or fear that the abuser will hurt, or even kill, their children

- Lack of the means to support themselves and/or their children financially or lack of access to cash, bank accounts, or assets

- Lack of having somewhere to go (i.e., no friends or family to help, no money for hotel, shelter programs are full or limited by length of stay)

- Fear that homelessness may be their only option if they leave

- Religious or cultural beliefs and practices may not support divorce or may dictate outdated gender roles and keep the victim trapped in the relationship

- Belief that two parent households are better for children, despite abuse

7

Societal Barriers to Escaping a Violent Relationship

∞

In addition to individual obstacles victims face when escaping violent relationships, society in general presents barriers. These include:

- A victim's fear of being charged with desertion, losing custody of children, or joint assets.

- Anxiety about a decline in living standards for themselves and their children.

- Reinforcement of clergy and secular counselors of "saving" a couple's relationship at all costs, rather than the goal of stopping the violence.

- Lack of support to victims by police officers and law enforcement who may treat violence as a "domestic dispute," instead of a crime where one person is physically attacking another person. Often, victims of abuse are arrested and charged by law enforcement even if they are only defending themselves against the batterer.

- Dissuasion by police of the victim filing charges. Some dismiss or downplay the abuse, side with the abuser, or do not take the victim's account of the abuse seriously.

- Reluctance by prosecutors to prosecute cases. Some may convince the abuser to plead to a lesser charge, thus further endangering victims. Additionally, judges rarely impose the maximum sentence upon convicted abusers. Probation or a fine is much more common.

- Despite the issuing of a restraining order, there is little to prevent a released abuser from returning and repeating abuse.

- Despite greater public awareness and the increased availability of housing for victims fleeing violent partners, there are not enough shelters to keep victims safe.

- Some religious and cultural practices that stress; that divorce is forbidden.

- The socialization of some made to believe they are responsible for making their relationship work. Failure to maintain the relationship equals failure as a person.

- Isolation from friends and families, either by the jealous and possessive abuser, or because they feel "ashamed" of the abuse and try to hide signs of it from the outside world. The isolation contributes to a sense that there is nowhere to turn.

- The rationalization of the victim that their abuser's behavior is caused by stress, alcohol, problems at work, unemployment, or other factors.

- Societal factors that teach women to believe their identities and feelings of self-worth are contingent upon getting and keeping a man.

- Inconsistency of abuse. During non-violent phases, the abuser may fulfill the victim's dream of romantic love. The victim may also rationalize that the abuser is basically good until something bad happens and they have to "let off steam."

8

The Faces of Abuse

∞

Do you think that you could recognize an abuser or victim when you saw them? What does he or she look like? They look like you and I.

Ray Rice is a former NFL player who was caught on video in 2014 in an elevator, punching and dragging his then fiancé; that caused her to be knocked unconscious for an extended period of time[1].

In light of the elevator video footage, Ray Rice was brought up on charges of domestic violence which was dismissed after a long courtroom ordeal. Due to these charges, he resigned from the Baltimore Ravens. The video became a media nightmare for him. Had there not been any video footage of the actual abuse; would anyone know that he was an abuser? No.

Travis Browne a UFC heavyweight was also accused of domestic violence by his ex-girlfriend in October 2014. The ex-girlfriend stated that she had been living with abuse for some time and that Travis allegedly caused several bruises all over her body, she was tired of the abuse and wanted people to know. [2]She posted a collage of pictures of the bruises on the social media site, Instagram. With many responses on Instagram, in regards to the photos', she admitted that leaving the abusive relationship with Travis was one of the hardest things she'd ever done.

In 2004, actress Diane Lane was alleged to have been the victim of domestic abuse after accusing her husband Josh Brolin of attacking her. However, she later dropped the charges against him. She had phoned police claiming he hit her during an argument at their Los Angeles home and Brolin was arrested that night for spousal battery. At the time, their spokeswomen said: "There was a misunderstanding at their home… she did not want to press charges… they are embarrassed the matter went this far."[3]

Former President Bill Clinton is a testament to a man's willpower that he can become one of the most powerful men in the world even though he grew up surrounded by domestic violence. When the former U.S. President was just 8 years old his mother married Roger Clinton, a car dealer from Arkansas and also an alcoholic. Life wasn't all rosy for the young Bill, and was – according to his autobiography – frequently marred by his stepfather's violent outbursts. It's said that, at the age of 15, Bill warned Roger never to hit his mother or half-brother ever again. In a later interview with *Time* magazine, Clinton recalled what a dramatic moment standing up to him had been.[4]

Oscar-winning actress Halle Berry is a fierce campaigner against domestic violence, having seen it firsthand. In 2004 she admitted to having been hit so hard by one of her ex-boyfriends that she lost the hearing in her right ear. Berry has never disclosed the identity of her attacker. She recently revealed that her mother was also the victim of domestic abuse, so when it happened to her, the actress knew it was time to get out of the relationship.[5]

Mariah Carey has hinted about her suffering abuse a few times in the past. In 2009 Mariah Carey came out and admitted she had been the victim of emotional and mental abuse. The mega-star was promoting a film which touches on the subject and said domestic abuse was not a new thing to her. Carey then married music mogul Tommy Mottola in 1993; they divorced 5 years later. The singer told Larry King: "Abuse has several categories… emotionally, mentally, in other ways. It's scary. I just think you get into a situation and you feel locked in… For me to really get out of it was difficult because there was a connection that was not only a marriage, but a business where the person was in control of my life."[6]

R&B star Rihanna has spoken publicly about the abuse she suffered from her ex-boyfriend. The singer was allegedly assaulted by Chris Brown and had visible bruises on her face. Brown handed himself in to police and issued a statement saying he was "sorry and saddened" and was seeking counseling. It turns out that Brown may have been subjected to violence himself after it was revealed his mother had been physically abused by his stepfather.[7]

The late Whitney Houston and Bobby Brown's turbulent relationship is well documented, but even though the rumors were that Bobby used to hit Whitney, she actually claimed it was the other way round. In an interview with the *Associated Press*, the singing star said: "Contrary to belief, I do the hitting, he doesn't. He has never put his hands on me. We are crazy for one another. I mean crazy in love, love, love, love, love. When we're fighting, it's like that's love for us. We're fighting for our love." Brown, however, was later arrested in 2003 for misdemeanor battery; several years after Whitney said this. The pair eventually divorced after 15 years of marriage in 2007.[8]

Tina Turner's violent marriage with Ike Turner is well known, largely thanks to the film based on her life, *"What's Love Got To Do With It.* In the film the singer suffered severe beatings, was raped and had cigarettes stubbed out on her body. Her husband Ike is portrayed as a violent, controlling sociopath, and when Tina's autobiography was published, Ike actually admitted that the book was largely accurate. The pair was married for 16 years before Tina had the courage to leave. Ike is now deceased.[9]

The individuals listed here are like anyone else; they just happen to be in the public eye when it came to the accusation and or charges of abuse. Their faces should be a sign that you really would not be able to recognize an abuser when you saw one. The abuser looks just like any once else. An abuser could be an NFL player, UFC heavyweight, celebrity, pastor, judge, teacher or even a police officer; no one is exempt. Abusers come from all walks of life.

If those in the public eye were not exposed by television or social media, would anyone know that they experienced any form of domestic abuse? This is usually the issue in abuse cases, the women don't share with anyone that they are being abused or she doesn't recognized that she is being abused because she is usually in love with the abuser and will make excuses about what has happened.

9

National Statistic

∞

Every nine seconds in the US, a woman is assaulted or beaten. On average, nearly twenty people per minute are physically abused by an intimate partner in the United States. During one year, this equates to more than ten million women and men. One in three women and one in four men have been victims of [some form of] physical violence by an intimate partner within their lifetime. One in five women and one in seven men have been victims of severe physical violence by an intimate partner in their lifetime. One in seven women and one in eighteen men have been stalked by an intimate partner during their lifetime to the point in which they felt very fearful or believed that they or someone close to them would be harmed or killed.

On a typical day, there are more than 20,000 phone calls placed to domestic violence hotlines nationwide. The presence of a gun in a domestic violence situation increases the risk of homicide by 500%. Intimate partner violence accounts for fifteen percent of all violent crime. Women between the ages of eighteen and twenty-four are most commonly abused by an intimate partner. Nineteen percent of domestic violence involves a weapon. Domestic victimization is correlated with a higher rate of depression and suicidal behavior. Only thirty-four percent of people who are injured by intimate partners receive medical care for their injuries.

RAPE

One in five women and one in seventy-one men in the United States have been raped in their lifetime. Almost half of female 46.7% and male 44.9% victims of rape in the United States were raped by an acquaintance. Of these, 45.4% of female rape victims and 29% of male rape victims were raped by an intimate partner.

STALKING

Nineteen- point one million women and 5.1 million men in the United States have been stalked in their lifetime. 60.8% of female stalking victims and 43.5% men reported being stalked by a current or former intimate partner.

HOMICIDE

A study of intimate partner homicides found that 20% of victims were not the intimate partners themselves, but family members, friends, neighbors, persons who intervened, law enforcement responders, or bystanders and 72% of all murder-suicides involve an intimate partner; 94% of the victims of these murder suicides are female.

CHILDREN AND DOMESTIC VIOLENCE

One in fifteen children, are exposed to intimate partner violence each year and 90% of these children are eyewitnesses to this violence.

ECONOMIC IMPACT

Victims of intimate partner violence lose a total of 8.0 million days of paid work each year. The cost of intimate partner violence exceeds $8.3 billion per year. Between 21-60% of victims of intimate partner violence lose their jobs due to reasons stemming from the abuse. Between 2003 and 2008, 142 women were murdered in their workplace by their abuser, 78% of women killed in the workplace during this timeframe.

PHYSICAL/MENTAL IMPACT

Women abused by their intimate partners are more vulnerable to contracting HIV or other STI's due to forced intercourse or prolonged exposure to stress. Studies suggest that there is a relationship between intimate partner violence and depression and suicidal behavior. Physical, mental, and sexual and reproductive health effects have been linked with intimate partner violence including adolescent pregnancy, unintended pregnancy in general, miscarriage, stillbirth, intrauterine hemorrhage, nutritional deficiency, abdominal pain and other gastrointestinal problems, neurological disorders, chronic pain, disability, anxiety and post-traumatic stress disorder (PTSD), as well as non-communicable diseases such as hypertension, cancer and cardiovascular diseases. Victims of domestic violence are also at higher risk for developing addictions to alcohol, tobacco, or drugs.

Interpersonal violence and abuse, especially between relatives and domestic partners, are leading causes of morbidity and mortality. Family physicians and other professionals who provide primary care health services must deal with acute presentations and chronic sequel of this epidemic. Many victims of abuse hesitate to seek help, while those who batter are often difficult to identify.

Medical management of patients in abusive relationships can be frustrating. Evaluating injury patterns, understanding factors that increase the risk for violence and making use of specific interview questions and techniques will aid family physicians in the difficult task of assessing and managing patients living in abusive partnerships.

Family violence usually results from the abuse of power or the domination and victimization of a physically less powerful person by a physically more powerful person. Other factors that create or maintain a power differential, such as unequal financial resources, family connections or health status, can also foster situations in which the more powerful person exerts inappropriate control or intimidation over the less powerful person. Any misuse of power; especially that which involves physical violence or psychological intimidation, constitutes abuse.

A perpetrator is a person who performs or permits the actions that constitute abuse or neglect. The term "batterer" refers more specifically to a perpetrator who engages in physical violence. It should be noted that, although the most familiar constellation for partner violence is one in which the (current or ex-) husband or boyfriend is the perpetrator and the wife or girlfriend is the victim, partner abuse also occurs in homosexual relationships and in heterosexual relationships in which men are the victims. In most cases it is the woman that is the victim but there are cases where men are also the victim, just not as common.

Domestic violence damages physical and emotional health and can have long lasting negative impacts across a wide range of health, social and economic outcomes. Domestic violence and intellectual development of the child and young person and has a major impact on the family. Identification of need and early intervention/work with families can significantly reduce risk of ongoing harm and is important not only for the wellbeing of the child but to the health and well being of the children and families affected. The guidance aims to increase knowledge within the field and support improved integration and partnership working with others who have an interest in preventing, working in and identifying domestic violence and abuse, and supporting those affected.

Programs to identify victims of violence and providing effective care and support are critical. This includes awareness screening tools and the training of medical staff. Domestic violence can be prevented. There is a wide array of strategies that can be used to address the risk factors for and promote protective factors across the life course. Interventions that develop parenting skills, support families and strengthen relationships between parents and children can have long-lasting preventive benefits. They prevent child abuse and improve child behavior, reducing children's risk of involvement in domestic violence later in life.

10

Personal Stories of Abuse

∞

Abuse usually isn't consistent or constant. In between, you become a normal couple. The stories you will read here will explain why these women stayed in their abusive relationships in their own words. If you notice, they are in a variety of age groups, showing here that domestic violence has no specific age prejudice. You will also find that they each had a different reason for staying. A male perspective is noted as well to show another side of the abuse.

Jenny 41 years old

Why didn't you just leave?' That is the question that everyone asks. I don't think you can really know until you are in that person's shoes. For me, I was in love. If I needed to suffer to be with my soul mate, so be it. Love is meant to hurt, right?

I was divorced and had two children from my first marriage when I met him. He had been married twice before. We moved quickly, and within six months we were living together. One night he went out with some friends and didn't come home. The next morning, when he finally walked in the door, I angrily asked him where he spent the night. He didn't even answer me; he just hit me in the face.

I was stunned. At the time, I didn't really grasp what had happened. I backed up and went into my daughter's room. At 3 years old, she was old enough to tell I was hurt. I minimized it to her and rationalized it to myself. *"He was tired. He didn't mean it"*. Later on, he was very apologetic and I swept the incident under the rug. I wasn't in a great place with my own self-esteem. My prior husband was verbally abusive towards me and had torn down my confidence. I felt lucky to have a new boyfriend who was, for the most part, good to me. I didn't want to lose him over one mistake.

Things returned to normal for half a year. Then he hit me again, and then apologized. The abuse followed a pattern: He would be loving and sweet for about six months; then he would blow up and hit me. I always thought each time was the last. And I became convinced it was up to me to save him from himself.

I believed I could love the abuse out of him. I thought if I were a good enough girlfriend, if I just loved him enough, he wouldn't want to hurt me again. It was almost a sick game in my head that I thought I could conquer. *"I am going to make him not want to abuse me. I will love him so much he won't hurt me anymore".* I didn't necessarily think I could change him. I thought I could make him so much more in love with me that it would click; he wouldn't want to hurt me.

I romanticized my role. I would be the one woman who was strong enough to teach him not to abuse. I would be the savior, the hero, the woman who stood by him despite the rough times. We, the survivors, we think that our abusers are going to have this 'aha' moment; the day they realize what they are doing to the women who love them. Every day we're hoping it's that day. I got stuck on the fact that he could be a good man when he wasn't abusing. I wanted that man, the kind, sweet, funny man; all the time. I thought he was capable of being that man. I got just enough of those good days to stay.

Five years into the relationship, I got pregnant. I thought he wouldn't hit me while I was carrying our child, but I was wrong. I went into labor with a black eye. Not one doctor asked me what it was from. After our son was

born, I thought things would be OK. *"We had a new baby. He'll be happy"*.
But that year turned out to be the worst.

He was drinking alcohol and using a lot of prescription drugs, and he
started to have schizophrenic episodes. He would self-medicate to alleviate
his high anxiety, using Xanax and alcohol, which always made him worse.
He had episodes of paranoia, and he'd accuse me of having the FBI put
cameras in the house to catch him abusing. The paranoia would pass, but it
was unpredictable. When he went out in public, I always had to be there to
make sure nothing happened.

Around my son's first birthday, we went to a concert in our
hometown. Things had been good, and we planned on having a nice night out
together. But the concert was small and crowded, and his anxiety started to
grow. He took 8 milligrams of Xanax. Then he started to fall asleep, so he
drank to stay awake. He said he was going to the bathroom and never came
back. When I went looking for him, I found management looking after him.
They told me to take him home and walked him to my car.

When we started driving, it looked like he was going to be sick, so I
pulled over to the curb. I reached across and I pushed the door open, turning
his body so he was facing out of the car. But he didn't recognize that the car

had stopped, and he thought I was trying to push him out of a moving vehicle. He accused me of trying to kill him and went ballistic.

He shut the door and swung with his right hand. I felt my cheekbone break. Within the first few seconds, he broke all the bones in the left side of my face and broke my nose. I knew if I didn't get away from him, there was a good chance I would die. I got in the back seat, I don't even know how. He got back there too. I was trying to roll down the windows. He kept grabbing my hands, hitting and biting me. He had me upside down. My neck and my head were almost under the driver's seat. He got on top of me and put his hands around my throat.

I was adamant that I didn't want to die. I had a 1-year-old and pre-teens. Somehow, I was able to get my foot on his chest and kick him away. I rolled the window down and screamed for help.

After that assault, I was in the ICU for four days. I had to have reconstructive surgery on my face. I still have tons of medical problems because of that night. He went to prison for seven years. He's out now. He has a girlfriend, I'm told.

It took that incident for me to say "that's enough." During my recovery, I made a list of all the reasons I stayed. I had 25. I was strong enough to stick it out. I wasn't ready to leave him. *"This is going to be this great story; I took this abusive man and turned him into a loving husband".* In my mind, he didn't know any better. Which is the dumbest thing; when you're 35 years old, you know beating your wife is not OK.

We rationalize until we can't rationalize anymore. When you are in the middle of it, you'll do anything to make them happy. I was so naïve that I didn't realize; no matter how much I loved him, he was always going to abuse me. Men don't outgrow being abusers.

Lavette

It wasn't until the end of my relationship with my ex-husband that things turned physical. When I realized that one of us was going to die, I knew I needed to leave.

I met him in college in the early '90s. He was the captain of the football team. From early on, he was very controlling and verbally and emotionally abusive. "You're stupid," he'd say. "No one else is going to want to be with you." It was my first adult relationship, and I didn't realize love wasn't meant to feel like that.

In the summer of 2009, it all went downhill. The verbal assaults turned physical. It started off with yelling and pushing, something thrown in my direction to assert his dominance. Then the pushing got harder. I got pushed to the ground. The thing he threw at me would actually hit me.

We had a birds' nest on our front porch and the birds were pooping all over the place. He decided he was going to spray the nest and kill the baby birds. My son was crying; he didn't want the birds to die. I decided to leave for the night. He flew into this rage and from the look in his eyes. I just knew that something was different.

He grabbed me by my hair and pulled me back into the house. He ordered our two kids to go upstairs. Once we were inside, he started punching me. We were in the laundry room and he grabbed shoes and boots and used them to hit me in the face. He jumped on my ribcage and cracked my rib. He strangled me until I saw stars. I was sure I was going to die. He pulled me into the living room and pointed his gun at me for hours. He loaded and unloaded it, ranting about what was wrong with me.

The next morning, the first thing he said was that I owed him an apology for, almost making him kill me. He didn't let me leave the house for three days because of all the bruises. After I was allowed to leave the house again, he warned me that if I told anyone or left him, he would "hunt" me down. He was going to shoot me. He was going to paralyze me. He was going to throw acid on my face. He was going to slit my throat.

It worked. I didn't tell a single person for five months. I knew if I did leave, he was capable of following through with the threats he was making. I was paralyzed with fear. Before the severe physical abuse, my reasons for staying were different. I thought I could still try to make the relationship work, and that it was better for the kids to have both parents. I talked myself into putting up with his behavior. But once the physical abuse accelerated, it was pure fear that kept me there. And that fear kept me silent for a long time.

Nikki 41 years old

My ex-husband was physical. I knew I needed to leave when I realized that one of us was going to die. I came to an epiphany. I realized that either he was going to kill me or I was going to kill him. I was always on edge, planning how to defend myself if he attacked me with a gun.

62

I broke my silence and told my mom what was happening. We quickly began making an exit plan. My mom opened up a bank account for me and I started putting money into it. When I was at work, I would go online and research resources. On my lunch break, I'd run home and take little things I knew I needed; personal items, clothes, photos and bring them to my mom's house. I made copies of all my important documents and put them back in their place. In the three weeks between when I told her and when I fled, we made all the preparations we could.

In November, I filed for a protection order. The day it was going to be served, I picked my kids up from school and took off to my sister's in Canada. I knew it was too dangerous to be near him after leaving. He was completely blindsided. He thought he was 100 percent in control of me, and that he would have that control forever. But he was wrong. I escaped. When I returned to our town a few weeks later, I had a new place to live. I never returned to him.

It's important to emphasize here that I did exactly what people say you should do. I left. I contacted a domestic violence resource center. I made a safety plan. I filed a restraining order. I found somewhere else to live. My employer moved me to a new building so my ex couldn't find me.

But still I wasn't safe. Actually, things got much worse. People always say, "Why don't you just leave?" They fail to understand that leaving doesn't necessarily stop the abuse. Women are at the highest risk of being killed when they leave their abusive partners. Leaving means; opening yourself up to incredible danger.

Once he lost his sense of control over me, things escalated. He immediately began stalking me. He would drive by my house. Call me over and over and describe how he would kill me. The protection order did nothing to stop him. I can't count how many times he violated it. When I would call the police, they seemed almost annoyed. If you haven't been assaulted, they'd say, there's nothing we can do. Lots of times, they wouldn't even come.

When he would get pulled into court for a violation, the judge would just give him a lecture. He's a great actor and he knew how to say the right things. He had been a police officer for about a year, and that got him a lot of second chances. He was arrested multiple times for aggravated stalking. But as soon as he was released, it would start again.

One time, I came in to make a police report after a particularly scary incident, and the officer asked me why I was there. I told him, and he said to me: "Well, what did you do? There will always be two sides of the story." I was in tears. This was after a year of being threatened and stalked, and I was being blamed? But then the officer noticed something outside the window. "What kind of car does your husband drive?" he asked me. "A black Toyota," I said. My ex was idling outside. At that point, a light bulb went on in the cop's head.

Eventually he went to prison for aggravated stalking. He's there now. Since he's been inside, he has told inmates that he is planning to kill me as soon as he gets out and that they will see him on the news one day soon. He was also caught trying to solicit inmates to murder me for $50,000. He will be eligible for parole in 12 months.

It's a horrible way to have to live your life, always looking over your shoulder. Even though I know he's incarcerated, I'm still worried. What if someone is dumb enough to think he will pay them to kill my kids and me? What will happen when he gets out of prison? How long will it be before he comes for me or my children? I live in a constant state of high anxiety. I'm always aware of my surroundings and who the people are around me and the closest exit out of any building. I left him, but I'm still terrified. No one should have to live like this.

Gabrielle 25 years old

We had mutual friends on Facebook and I sent him a friend request. I was 22 and thought he was cute. He was the same age and as I soon found out; he was about to spend a year in jail for an incident involving a former girlfriend. But it was easy to overlook his past when he told me his version of the story. I fell for him hard. For the whole year he was in jail, we dated. He painted a pretty picture of what our life would be like once he was out.

When he came home, things seemed OK at first. He never put his hands on me, except in a loving way. But he was verbally abusive; belittling, name-calling, a lot of manipulation. It didn't take long before his extreme jealousy led to blowout fights. More than once, he accused me of cheating on him while he was in jail. We broke up and got back together a few times.

One night I was at my job at a hotel and he wouldn't stop calling me. He got worked up and threatened to throw rocks through the hotel windows. I was scared he would do it, so I told my boss, who called the cops. The following day; my boss gave me an ultimatum; get a restraining order so he doesn't come here anymore, or quit.

I got the restraining order and didn't talk to him for three weeks. But then my friend told me she saw him at the courthouse and he was so sorry about everything. I dropped the restraining order and went back to him. At the time, I believed I was pregnant with his child, and I loved him. I didn't want to raise the kid alone. Later, I found out it was a false alarm.

He had struggled with heroin in the past, but he was sober when we got back together. For one month, things were good. We took long bike rides, had ice cream dates; acted just like a normal couple but that all came to a screeching halt in 2013.

One summer night, he picked me up at work and began accusing me of being unfaithful again. I went to text someone and he flipped out. He pulled off the road and threw my phone out the window. When I tried to get out of the car, he grabbed my hair and violently yanked my head into his lap. He told me not to ever get out of the car unless he said to. I was in shock. He'd never put his hands on me before.

Once he calmed down, he said he needed me to take a lie detector test to prove I wasn't a cheater. He told me I was the problem, I was the reason he was so angry; I was to blame for all our problems. I thought he was

67

being ridiculous, but I agreed to take the test, because I wanted to be with him.

That night was when everything turned bad. We came home, had sex and started taking a shower together. Out of nowhere, he began hitting me across the face. I fell, knocking over shampoo bottles. I don't remember what I said to him or what he said to me, I just remember seeing his hand coming at my face. I tried to walk out and he grabbed me by my hair again, yelling that I wasn't allowed to leave any place without his permission.

I went into the bedroom and stood in my towel trying to process what happened. It's disorientating, being unexpectedly hit by someone who says they love you. I didn't know how to react. He followed me into the bedroom and pushed me on the bed, wrapping his hands around my neck. He strangled me until I stopped struggling. I don't remember how long it lasted or how it ended, but it finally did.

The next day, we were out for a drive when he got an idea. He was going to make me take heroin with him, so I knew how he felt. I'd never used drugs before. I don't even smoke cigarettes. He pulled the car off onto a dirt road, injected himself and then injected me as I desperately begged him not to. Within minutes, I was slumped over in the car seat.

That was the beginning of the most harrowing week in my life. What I endured over the next five days can only be described as hell. He injected me with heroin every day. It made me throw up constantly. At first, he would let me throw up in the woods, but soon he stopped letting me out of his sight and made me vomit into an old T-shirt in his car. I was his captive.

He started brutally beating me, taking me into the woods to hit me with a belt, and told me over and over how he was going to kill me. At one point, I remember getting out of the shower and seeing my naked body in the mirror. I turned my body, maybe to wring out my hair, and caught a glimpse of the bruises. I couldn't believe what I saw. I was still in complete shock that someone who I believed loved me, and who I loved, could do that to me. When I got upset about my bruises, he said I looked sexy all beat up. I was defeated.

On the third night, he thought of a new way to destroy me. He pulled out a camera and forced me to give his pit bull oral sex while he videotaped it. He said he wanted to prove what kind of cheater I was. He told me he would use the video to blackmail me if I left him or told anyone about the abuse. He would make sure everyone saw the video, including my mother. It gave him that much more power and control over me. That night, I felt like I

69

was stuck with him no matter what. I was trapped. I felt like his property. I was literally just his punching bag.

His abuse progressed very quickly. It all happened in one week. He drugged me, he tried to kill me; he raped me. I had bruises all over my face and all over my rear end. I believe he would have killed me. If not with his own two hands, then with the drugs. If he gave me too much, I would have overdosed. I'm surprised I didn't.

After five days of brutal abuse, I was at work when he called me and told me to quit my job because we were going out of town. My boss saw me crying. She asked what was going on and offered to help me. That's when I decided I needed to get out. I went to the police station. The next day I pressed charges. He got six years. He's now in jail until 2019.

People always ask why I stayed. During the court proceedings, the defense attorney asked me over and over why I didn't just leave. That was the moment I broke down and ran out of the courtroom in tears. The truth is; I didn't think things could get much worse than they already were. I was in a complete daze, drugged, sick to my stomach, full of shame, hurt and pain. He did everything he could to beat me down until I felt worthless. It almost worked, almost.

As hard as it is to accept what happened, it's easier the more I talk about it. I know that I shouldn't have to feel ashamed about what happened to me. The way I look at the whole process of leaving, I am one day further away from the abuse I endured, and all the feelings I felt during that week. I am one day closer to reaching happiness and success in life. It's a part of my past, but it's done defining me.

Ashley

I met Benny when I was 15 and he was 16. He was very good looking and many girls wanted to be his girlfriend. He never had many friends who were guys and he wasn't into sports. At first, he was really nice to me and always invited me over to his house after school. He really liked cars and had a place set up in his Dad's garage where he worked on a broken-down car that his uncle had given him. Most afternoons after school, I would get into trouble with my Mom because Benny made me stay with him while he worked on his car. When I told him that I had to leave, he told me that I wanted to rush home because I didn't care about him and that there were lots of girls who would want to hang around him.

After a few months, he didn't want me to do anything with my friends. He was possessive and jealous and would make fun of anyone who

71

was my friend. He made me feel guilty if I even talked to someone at school, even when he wasn't around, which wasn't very often. He told me that he didn't like what I wore and told me what I should wear to school. He was always moody, but after a while it made me feel really uncomfortable. He forced me to have sex with him in his Dad's garage. I told him that I loved him, but that it didn't seem like he loved me. I was afraid I would get pregnant and told him that I wanted to wait. He slapped me and said never to say anything like that again. He told me that he would decide if I would get pregnant or not. I told him that wasn't the way it worked and he slapped me again, harder and twisted my arm behind my back. I was afraid to tell my Mom or anyone what happened, but I stopped going over to his house after school.

After almost every class, he would stand outside the doorway and grab my arm when I came out and whisper in my ear that I better listen to him or something bad was going to happen to me. I didn't know what to do and I tried to avoid him, but it seemed like he was always there waiting for me or watching me. He sent me text messages all day and all night long. Sometimes he pleaded with me not to break up with him. Sometimes he would send me threats or text me, "I know what you're doing right now."

One day a teacher saw him grab me and I guess I looked pretty shook up. She waited until he walked away and then motioned for me to come into her classroom. We walked into the back where she had a little office and she closed the door. I didn't even know her very well, but I started to cry. I couldn't help it. I said that nothing was wrong, but she just waited for me to stop crying and didn't ask me any questions. I said I had to go and I got up to leave. That's when she said words that I remembered ever since: "You don't deserve to be treated like that." I knew she was right, but I just couldn't see it before she said those words out loud.

It took me about two weeks before I had the courage to go back to talk to her again, this time after school when no one else was around. She said that I didn't have to be with Benny if I didn't want to and I said I knew that, but I didn't know how to get out. He said he was going to really hurt me. She explained to me some things called dating violence. She talked about some things that my Mom and I might want to think about. I knew I had to tell my Mom. When I did, she helped me understand what was going on. I threw away my cell phone and didn't get another one until after I had changed schools. I had to get away from Benny, and I'm glad I did. I don't ever want to have to worry about leaving class and having someone waiting for me. I am 17 now and will graduate from high school this year. I know

now how different my life would have been right now if I had stayed around Benny.

Chrissy

For seven years, I was afraid to go to sleep at night and for seven years there were barely any nights that I got a full night's sleep. My husband worked long hours, with a lot of overtime. I rarely saw him in the daytime, but the times he was around, things were okay. But at night, he would terrorize me, waking me up after I fell asleep, yelling at me, calling me names and threatening to hurt me. I asked him what was going on. I asked him what I had done to cause him to act this way. I didn't understand his behavior. During the first year of our marriage, these episodes were very infrequent and I could not figure out any reason for him to act like that towards me. He wasn't drinking or on drugs that I could tell. I kept asking him what was wrong.

After we had our first child, the nights became worse. I was a wreck and between my husband and the baby, I wasn't getting any sleep. I was unable to go back to work at the end of my maternity leave and I lost my job. My husband got worse after that. He told me that I was worthless and asked what good was I if I couldn't even hold down a job. Some nights I would go to sleep and he would punch me in the neck or head to wake me. Once he held a pillow over my head until I couldn't breathe. I think I lost consciousness. Another time, he tried to choke me. When I locked the bedroom door to keep him out, he broke the door lock and the next day, he took the door completely off its hinges. I felt like I was losing my mind and I knew it was from the lack of sleep. I started going to my Mother's house with the baby to sleep in the daytime while he was at work. When he found out, he smashed my head into the wall so hard it left a mark in the wall.

One morning, I was trying to make coffee and I saw something on TV. It was an interview with a woman who worked at a local domestic violence center. The things she was saying all began to make sense. Some of the things she described sounded like me. There was a toll-free number on the bottom of the screen. I didn't call the number that day, but the more I thought about it, the more I wanted to find out about the program I had heard about on TV.

Now, I get a good night's sleep because I did make the call to the toll-free domestic violence hotline. Over several months, they provided me with resources and a friendly voice when I needed to talk. I began to understand that my husband's behavior was not a result of something that I did. I learned it wasn't my fault. I attended a support group and learned that there are other women who were going through things that were familiar to me. When I was strong enough, the staff from the Center helped me with a plan for my safety. I wanted to make a decision to leave, but I was having a hard time. I loved him, but I had to get away. I started worrying about whether he was going to hurt the baby. Every time I changed my mind about whether to go or stay, my Advocate at the domestic violence center was a friendly voice. I could talk with her and she would always listen. I felt like I could tell her what was going on and she didn't judge me. She always told me she was there for me, no matter what I decided. When I made the decision to leave, she supported me.

Occasionally, I still wake up in the middle of the night, but it's not because someone has punched me awake. I can now go back to sleep knowing that for the first time in a long time, I am safe.

Tamron Hall

Former NBC new anchor, Tamrom *Hall* tells the story of her healing and happiness after the brutal murder of her sister from domestic violence.

With its sleek, slate colored couches, modern art work in the regal white living room with the taxidermy peacock on display, Tamron Hall's sophisticated Manhattan apartment is a far cry from where she came from. We didn't have paved streets in my town, she says of growing up in rural Luling, Texas, with her mom, Mary, an educator, stepdad Clarence Newman Sr., an army sergeant and four siblings. The family didn't have much money, but we were rich in life and rich in love.

Hall, 45, was determined to make it as a journalist, attending Temple University and working in local news before getting national attention as an NBC anchor. In 2014 she became the today shows first-ever African American female co-anchor. Her success was haunted by a tragedy she kept private. In 2004 Hall's older sister Renate then 48, was murdered in her Houston home. The crime came after years of being in a relationship with an abusive man and remains unsolved. "No one deserves what happened to my sister, says Hall". For a long time I was hesitant about sharing our story, but screw that if it means I can save a life and help someone.

Her search for justice is rooted in the tight bond she shared with her sibling. Though the two were not blood related, we didn't use the words half or step, Hall says. We were family, when I needed advice, I asked my sister.

But their paths diverged. A young mom, her sister raised sons Damien, 41, and Leroy, 38, alone and struggled with alcohol before turning her life around and getting a promotion at the bank where she worked. She was smart and beautiful, Hall says. Still, she'd fall for men who took advantage of her.

Renate came to visit, bringing along a male companion; who Hall will not name out of fear of retaliation. One night I heard a commotion at my home and ran downstairs she recalls. My sister was standing there, stunned. A huge knot had already formed on the front of her head, and my den was in shambles. The man made excuses, but I immediately kicked him out. But Hall decided not to call the police. I was embarrassed, she now admits. I didn't want it to be in the paper; that some violent situation happened at Tamron Hall's house.

The next morning Hall was shocked to find that her sister had allowed the man back in. Enraged, she voiced her disapproval and cut off contact with Renate for a year, a decision she deeply regrets. I said to her, "what is wrong with you"? You are too beautiful, too smart; you can do better. All the things I said and done, I've now learned; were wrong, which I've learned from a domestic abuse advocate, but I did them all.

Renate's beaten body was found floating in her small backyard pool. My mom called me, inconsolable, says Hall. The night Renate was killed; she told my mom that she wanted out of the relationship. In a court hearing, Hall states, detectives identified the man as a person of interest; but due to the lack of evidence were unable to make an arrest. Hall hired a private investigator but who also came up empty; and that case is still open.

Hall struggled to move past guilt. We never fully reconnected, she says of Renate. I think she thought I still judged her. Hall found solace in Advocacy, with Renate's two sons and other family members. She began working with Safe Horizon and Day One, two groups fighting to end domestic violence. As host of the ID Channel's, *Deadline: Crime*, Hall hopes to help other families find closure.

The tragedy has made her cautious about relationships. I've been engaged a couple of times; thank God no one was abusive, she says. My friends call me the runaway bride. But she hopes to start a family one day, right now her focus is her career. I love my job and my relationship with the viewers, she says. It's a relationship that's grown stronger sense sharing Renate's a story. I got a private e-mail from an NBC colleague saying she'd left an abusive relationship and she wanted to thank me. I've been given the opportunity to make a difference. [10]

Lawrence

As a child, I lived in an environment where I was exposed to domestic violence but wasn't aware of what it was. I saw my father become physical with my mother when she wouldn't follow his strict instructions. My mother was one who was strong, had her own mind; her thoughts and opinions ran deep. She was raised by a mother who taught her to always speak her mind. "Never let a man have total control over you". Because my mother was raise with this mindset, it often caused conflict in the relationship with my father; who was taught to be in control at all times.

To maintain a level of economic control, my father set rules in regards to the finances; even though my mother worked, he would set an allowance for her but in doing so this caused her to become angry and resentful towards him. The resentment led to what began as normal conversation and turned into an argument. Her defiance caused my father to feel disrespected and he would become angry.

This aggression made him feel forced to become physical with her to keep her in her respected place. He would use pushing or slapping to insure that he could regained control of her. If those things didn't work alone, he made the presence of a gun known to her to place a level of fear. I never saw him pull a gun on my mother but I remember him telling me as an eight year old boy; that if anyone ever disrespected me, that I should get the gun and use it if I needed to.

I remember those words came back to haunt my father, when he and my uncles were gathered at our home for a guys' night. There was drinking and conversations that got a little out of control. I came in to see what was going on, to be told that this was no place for a little boy. The tone my father took with me made me feel disrespected. I became upset, and I went for the gun. I came back to the room where all the men were, with the gun in hand. I confronted my father, pointed the gun at him. He asked me son, where did you get a gun? In disbelief because I was seemingly too small to reach it in the location it was stored. I proceeded to tell him that I felt disrespected. I explained to him that he told me if I've felt disrespected by anyone, that I could go for the gun; so I did. My father said, I didn't mean me son. As I look back at that situation, I realized I was being conditioned to this type of violent behavior.

81

Under normal circumstances, my father was a charming husband and a loving father to my sister and I, but needed to be control of the family at all times. What I didn't realize is that watching my father's controlling and abusive behavior showed me how to behave, react and or respond to others when I was placed in certain situations that I saw my father in.

As a young child, I saw this as normal. Once I became a teenager, I started to behave with some of the same aggression towards others, as my father displayed with my mother. When I began to date and had a disagreement with my girlfriend; if she didn't agree with me, I would get angry and become physical in the same fashion as my father did with my mother.

The idea of a man managing and controlling his family goes way back in my family's history. From one generation to the next, the men in my family were taught to control the woman in the relationship. Therefore, I didn't know any different. The behavior I saw from my father was also displayed in relationships that my uncles were in as well.

By the time I reached young adulthood, all I knew to do with the women in my life, was to be sure that I maintain the same level of control in my relationships. If the women in my life weren't responsive in the way that was pleasing to me, I would give a warning and if the warning was disregarded or I've felt disrespected; then I would become violent. I would slap, push, emotionally and/or verbally abused them. At this time I didn't think anything was wrong.

As the result of me not understanding, that not any one person is another's property nor should they be controlled; it caused me to move from one relationship to the next, looking for that one person who would be responsive to me in the way I felt was satisfactory to my standards. When I've found that one young woman, it was usually one that was from a home that had seen the same type of physical violence displayed. Girls who had experienced violence between their parents would normally just assume the victim role and it made the relationship easier for me.

But as I reflect back; now that I am an adult, I realize that this behavior was in fact abusive. I did a lot of things, to a lot a women that I regret; if I could take some of those things back I would. Since I couldn't and I was faced with the realization of the level of emotional, financial, verbal and physical abuse that I may have caused some of the women in my life. I decided to give a few of them a call to apologize.

I also understand now that the emotional scars of my abuse lasted much longer than the physical abuse. When I made some of those phone calls, the women explained to me that I broke their confidence, self-esteem and self-worth and in doing so; this caused them to choose other men in their lives that were abusive on some level.

This revelation didn't come to me right away. Because I grew up with the mentality that power and control was what I was supposed to have at all times; when I found myself in situations in my intimate relationships or otherwise and I was not in control, I would become angry and ultimately violent. As a result of my violent behavior, I found myself in prison for fifteen years. In prison is where I had the revelation that my behavior was not acceptable in society. My mindset and behavior has to change. I now understand that my treatment of women was unwarranted. No woman deserves to be abuse in any way.

Today I own a business in which I can touch the lives of many men; young and old, and with every opportunity; I have conversations with them about relationships and the importance of love, affection, understanding, kindness, consideration and a woman's worth.

When I look at my mother, I see the long lasting results of her domestic violence and abuse. As a result of her abuse, she chose to raise my sister to be, what she felt was a strong woman but in fact caused my sister to become an abuser. Her abuse is verbal and emotional towards her husband and she doesn't recognize it as abuse. When abuse is not recognized, it is passed on as a learned behavior. For example: my sister now has daughters who respond in relationships the same as what they've observed all of their life therefore they are abusers to a degree.

This behavior is so ingrained that it has become perpetuated without any awareness. It spans over four generations. Trying to have the conversation with women in regards to abuse is different than having that conversation with men. Depending on where you find yourself when it comes to the topic of abuse; it may very well be a different conversation for women than men. In most cases the woman are the victim and has been abused by a man therefore the conversation is not easy to have. The woman is usually more sensitive because she has been hurt by abuse. When talking to men, who are customarily the abuser; they have a complete different outlook on what abuse is.

So I find myself trying to explain to the women in my family both sides of the coin when it comes to abuse. I understand a male's perspective because I've been the abuser, and I also understand a woman's perspective because I've had extensive conversations with a few that I previously abused. I have great remorse for it and had those conversations that were tough.

Tough in the sense that I had to admit that I had a problem but also explained the learned behaviors and changed the way I respond. My experience has given me a PhD in life. Would I do things differently if I could? Yes, but some of my experience was given to me in order for me to teach someone else how to avoid going through what I did. I am a better man for it.

Tonya

I started going to the domestic violence shelter for counseling. But I was just, "Ehh. Why should I do this? "I'm not going to sit here and tell you my business." I went to the shelter eight times. Eight! But there was always some reason that I went back to him. I wasn't ready. I was in denial.

Tonya shared her story; explaining that her partner beat her until she bled, set fire to her bed while she was sleeping, and used every weapon he could find to harm her. She did leave on several occasions, but returned again and again to the same person who hurt her so badly. At first glance, it is hard to imagine why a victim of domestic violence who is repeatedly beaten, degraded, and violated would voluntarily remain in the relationship with the abuser.

Thinking about why it may sometimes actually be adaptive to ignore abuse by a trusted person can help make sense of why victims of domestic violence often do not report abuse, under report the severity of ongoing violence, and return to or remain in abusive situations.

Domestic violence affects approximately one in five women world-wide and one in four women in the United States in their lifetime. It leaves physical scars from broken bones and increases the likelihood of developing illnesses from living in an intensely stressful environment for a prolonged period of time.

It leaves psychological scars from anxiety due to living in ongoing danger, and a shaken world view from having been betrayed by a trusted person. Among those whose lives are directly affected by domestic violence, the majority of victims eventually leave the relationship. But the leaving process can involve years of cycling out of, then back into the relationship.

When a person is abused by an intimate partner, she experiences a devastating betrayal committed by someone she once may have viewed as her closest ally. She may be further betrayed when the institutions and communities she turns to for support fail to validate her experience and fail to provide access to necessary resources.

To begin to understand how difficult it is for domestic violence victims to leave a relationship characterized by betrayal, it is imperative to listen to what victims and survivors have to say.

11

Men vs. Women Characteristics

∞

Abusive men are found among all races, socioeconomic classes and occupations. Though the characteristics for men and women are different; it has only been in the past few years have sufficient descriptions been gathered to allow some tentative listings of both the personality and environmental factors that an abuser brings into a relationship. The combination of the personality of the abuser and social influences can go a long way in predicting the likelihood of intimate partner violence.

Although men may infrequently be the victims of abuse, the relatively minor nature of injuries men receive, pales when compared to women. Due to the heavy imbalance toward the abuse of women and the lack of reliable description of victimized men, the focus is usually on the women.

Individuals who have experienced violence and abuse in their childhoods are more likely to grow up and become and abuser. Those who either observed their parents abuse each other or who were abused as a child are, more likely to engage in or have a tolerance for the use of violence. Not only does research show that violence begets violence but the evidence strongly suggests that the greater the frequency, the greater the chance the victim will grow up to be a violent partner or parent. A person who sees violence as the primary method of problem solving usually doesn't learn how to properly resolve conflict because problem solving was never observed.

Most men in American society are less capable than women in expressing their feelings with words. Abusive men have an especially hard time in expressing emotions other than anger; so feelings of anxiety, fear, frustration, and sometimes even affection are expressed in one way only, violent anger. Many of these men have sufficient verbal skills to function day to day but they do not have the ability to express what they think of feel when it comes to their partner. When a woman doesn't read her partners mind, he may interpret this as rejection or the lack of love from her and respond with violence. It has been suggested that men use their inexpressiveness as a power strategy to maintain a position of dominance.

Men who abuse their partner are usually very emotionally dependent on their partners. Their dependency is expressed through their need for nurturance, comfort, and constant reassurance. Abusive men act in controlling ways to exert power and to deny their own weakness. A major symptom is strong jealousy and possessive actions toward a partner. The jealousy is usually sexual in nature. The man will often accuse the woman of sexual relations with others. Often the jealousy is extended to family and friends. The man is a likely to spend a great deal of energy on monitoring his partner and their activities and making accusations. For example, it might be timing; how long it takes to get home from work, then calling to make sure she is on her way.

An abusive man lacks other supportive relationships and tends to only have superficial contact with anyone outside of his own family. When an abuser fears losing his partner it's possible for him to feel that physical violence is his only own recourse. Most abusers will promise to make any changes necessary to keep their partners after the abuse; some will even threatened suicide, although very few actually carry out the threat.

Studies indicate abusive men are generally nonassertive outside of the home, possess a low self-esteem and are depressed. Depression can result from

91

internalize anger, so it is very possible for some abusive men to ricochet between depressed non-assertiveness and aggression. Many times, the depression will be hidden under a tough guy exterior.

Many abusers are very dominating and demands control of almost every aspect of their partner's life. They expect to make all major decisions, they tend to become angry if their partners disagree or act independently. Oftentimes the abuser will monitor all of the partner's activities outside of the home. Some men will use their religious beliefs for support of his reasoning to abuse his partner. Whether Christian or not, the abuser expects his partner to fulfill her sex role, be responsible for the household, be submissive and subservient.

Men who abuse their partners have often been found to have problems with substance abuse, alcohol or drugs. It was reported that 67% of abusers are frequently abusing alcohol. It was also found that the abuse of alcohol is more likely to result in serious injuries to the woman. Although some form of substance abuse is usually present in abusive relationships, this does not mean that drug or alcohol abuse is necessarily causing the violence. The use of alcohol and drugs may often allow the abuser to avoid responsibility of his behavior. He will use the excuse, "I was drunk out of my mind and didn't know what I was doing". It is likely, substance abuse and intimate partner violence is related, and that both problems represent an inappropriate response to stress.

Economic stresses such as unemployment, underemployment, or high levels of job dissatisfaction have been found to be related to domestic violence. It has been reported only 15% of abusers were actually unemployed at the time of the abuse. Like alcohol, stress from unemployment has been used as an excuse for a man to hit. Financial problems are not the only stressors related to domestic violence. Any major event that would serve to upset the individual or his thought of equilibrium such as medical problems, discipline concerns with children or pregnancy can lead to violence.

Another major finding of domestic of violence is that social isolation raises the level of violence between couples. Physical isolation can also contribute says a social service agency, medical or educational help may be limited. Most people who undergo stress are able to turn to other family members, friends, neighbors, or their church for financial and emotional support. Many abusive couples lacked such a network. This isolation may have been self induced but can produce more stress and leads to more abuse.

Abused women often will come for help only when they believe their children are in danger. Hospital emergency room personnel reports abused individuals only show up for treatment when there is blood. The sight of blood seems to trigger a realization that there is personal danger involved. Even when they might be internal injuries, broken bones, many abused woman will not go to the hospital. They have lost touch with their physical boundaries, including the awareness of pain. For most victims, the abuse has become familiar and common. So it usually takes something significant to break the thinking pattern that abuse is a way of life; this is something the abused woman must accept. Unfortunately, the only thing that sometimes gets through to a victimized woman is the broken arm of a child.

Many abused wives seek help from their pastors or Christian counselors only to be told they should be more submissive and/ or sexually available to their husbands; the implications being that the wife is not an obedient Christian woman and that it is her fault her husband gets angry. This kind of counsel only serves to increase the guilt level and keeps the husband from taking responsibility for his actions.

Cultural or religious constraints regarding separation or divorce may deter the wife from seeking help. Fears of physical retaliation, economic loss and losing custody of their children create a paralysis and keep the wife locked into a vicious cycle.

The Christian wife has a higher level of commitment to keep the marriage together. She often cannot distinguish between the steps needed to get help for herself and her husband and the actual eventuality of divorce. Something significant has to happen in the life of the husband in order get him to recognize his needs and responsibility. Divorce should not have to be the only solution but abused wives tend to view the situation as all or nothing. She believes she only has two options. Either, stay in the abuse or leave and risk divorce. Neither extreme seems palatable, so she will take no action at all.

There are three phases to the abuse: there is the tension building phase, the acute violent episode phase, and the remorse phase. The tension building phase is a period of mounting stressors. There is a gradual escalation of incidents of irritation over such things as finances or the children. Some expression of dissatisfaction is present but often the frustrations are not dealt with directly. Those feelings are held inside where they become more intense. Communication and cooperation diminish as the husband and wife/ or partner tend to withdraw from each other. The abuser

95

may express dissatisfaction and hostility but not in an extreme form. The victim may attempt to placate the abuser, trying to please him, calm him down, and avoid further confrontations. The victim, at this point, tries not to respond to his hostile actions. She will tend to use some type of anger - reduction technique which often works for little while. This temporary reduction of hostility reinforces her belief that she can control her partner and/or husband and prevent things from getting worse. The tension continues to increase and the victim finds that she is unable to control the abuser's angry responses. Once this happens, the victim withdraws, not wanting things to get any worse.

The acute violence phase becomes inevitable unless there's some type of intervention. Sometimes the victim will precipitate the inevitable explosion so she can at least control where and when it occurs. This will allow her to take precautions and to minimize her injuries and pain. The abuser may also get drunk, anticipating a violent confrontation, this phase may last anywhere from 1 hour to several months. Sometimes, just before the violence occurs the abuser may withdraw and refuse to communicate.

After the explosive release of violence comes a period of relative calm in the remorse phase. Attention has been dissipated, at least until the next episode. The abuser may apologize profusely, try to help the victim, show kindness in remorse, and shower her with gifts and promises that it will never happen again. This behavior often comes out of a genuine sense of guilt over the harm inflicted, as well as fear of losing the partner. During this time, the abuser often believes that he will never allow himself to be that violent again.

The remorse phase provides the reinforcement for remaining in the relationship. Interviews done with abuse victims indicate that even if the abusive partner did not engage in observable loving-contrition behavior following the violent episode, the reduction of tension alone was sufficient reinforcement for the victim.

The level of intimacy during this "makeup" phase may be better than any other period in the lives of the couple. They may communicate feelings in the context of guilt and vulnerability that's usually not revealed. There may be a shift in power during this time. The victim may now feel protective of her abuser and that she is the stronger of the two. She now has gone from being comparatively powerless to powerful. If she were to make any statements or efforts to leave, the balance of power is even more evident. If the police, family, pastor, or mental health worker makes contact with the family during the early part of remorse phase they will likely meet with resistance. It is important to help the victim recognize the seriousness of the violence.

Recognition of the seriousness and prevalence of violence has been slow in coming to all sections of American society and the church is no exception. Courses in pastoral counseling do not normally deal with assault, incest or rape. On the other hand, many professionals have not had formal training in dealing with violence either. Clergy are often the first people a victim will contact. Pastors are one of the largest groups of professionals who could have an impact on domestic violence but they need to know how to help, rather than make things worse.

There are four possible outcomes following the violent episode. Three of these, result in restoration of calmness for a time and one leads to further crisis.

1. The first possible outcome is for the abuser to become very remorseful, guilty and ask his partner for forgiveness in either verbal or non-verbal ways. This is the typical sequence of events as described earlier. If the victim forgives, excuses, or avoids making an issue of the event, calmness is restored. Tension has

been reduced but the behaviors of both victim and offender that led to that reduction have been reinforced.

2. The abuser may not feel remorseful at all. He may believe that his violence was justified and necessary to establish control. If the victim accepts that state of affairs and acquiesces to the authority of her partner, whether out of fear or belief in her own wrongdoing, calmness is restored. The victim has yielded to the threats of her abuser and his behavior has been rewarded.

3. If the victim takes assertive action to either get help, threatens to leave, or establishes conditions for continuing the relationship, the couple may move toward improvements in the situation to restoration. This would probably be the ideal outcome, if it resulted in changes that stop the violence and improve the relationship.

4. In contrast, if the victim takes assertive action to change the occurrence of violence, the abuser may reject the proposed changes. The result in this case will be a crisis. The victim is no longer willing to subject herself to the threat of violence, but the abuser would not go along with her proposals. If the victim decides to leave, the abuser is made angrier by the decision; he

may try to stop her. Many times victims have been seriously harmed by a distraught abuser who couldn't handle his victim's departure.

If the victim demands that they; as a couple get counseling, or that the abuser join Alcoholics Anonymous or get other treatment, the abuser rejects such an opinion, and the situation continues in crisis.

The bedroom is the most likely place for a female to be killed. The conflict often occurs at night, when there is no place to go. The bathroom is the most frequently occupied room during the act of violence. It is demilitarized zone of the home and typically is the one room in the house that always has a lock. Often this room is used as a refuge for family members to avoid violence.

Couples most often engage in physical conflict between 6:00 pm and midnight. Violence is more frequent when neither partner works or when partners work on alternating shifts. At mealtime is a particularly dangerous time due to the accumulation of daily frustrations. The conflict is most likely to begin over the management of the children and money.

Violence is more conducive to weekends versus weekdays, holidays such as Christmas and New Year's Eve are also notable troubled times. There is a slight tendency for more violence to occur during warmer months. It is more likely for the violence to occur when the woman is pregnant. Note that as the frequency of the abusive episodes increase, the more severe they become.

12

Processing the Intervention

∞

The victim may request the help during or right after an act of violence. They may come to a counselor with another related concern; with careful questioning, they might reveal a need for an intervention because of crisis. A referral may come from a community agency such as an emergency shelter. The victim may have sought refuge in a shelter but wants her pastor to be involved. A member of the family may contact a pastoral counselor out of concern for the abuse victim.

It's important to remember that if a battered woman has been pushed by others into bringing the violence out into the open, she may be very ambivalent about taking action. Sometimes it is only when the violence is directed at the children that a mother will take the drastic action. It is important to be as accepting and comforting as possible. The abuse victim has already been physically and emotionally traumatized; she doesn't need to be put on the defensive by questions, such as "What did you do to set him off"?

The first step in intervention process is to determine what has motivated a family member to seek help. Very often the first person to contact is a pastor or counselor and that will be done by the victim or an adolescent child. There will be times when an abusive partner will initiate a contact, usually doing the remorseful phase, or after the victim has taken drastic action. It's important to take the situation seriously. Whatever your relationship to the person who seeks your help, listen to him or her carefully. Abuse should not be minimized. But both victims and abusers will tend to understate the extent of the abuse. **Above all, believe the woman has been abused**!

Sometimes a person will contact the pastor or counselor with a secondary to the crisis. You should always be alert for signs that could be indirect symptoms of abuse. Some of these indicators are:

- History of miscarriages
- History of or recent increase in prescriptions for tranquilizers
- History of or recent increase in excessive use of alcohol

- Repeated visits to the emergency room for medical treatment of injuries or illnesses

- Signs of ongoing stress, such as headaches, gastrointestinal ailments, or their "not feeling well' complaints

- Contacts with community mental health agencies or other psychiatric facilities

- Suicide attempts

- Nonprescription drug abuse

- Isolation from friends of family

- Reports of police intervention

- Reports of conflict with others outside of the home

- Description of abuser being moody or unpredictable

- Reference to abusive or violent history

When several of these symptoms are present, further questioning should be asked, about the possibilities of abuse. Their presence does not mean abuse is certain, only that you should investigate further. Again, Ask questions. If a woman comes to you and says things are pretty tense at our home; my husband\partner really lost his cool the other day, explore the details of the encounter; even if there are not any bruises. Ask if she has ever been hit and how often the outbursts occur. By asking questions, you show that you're taking the situation seriously.

Intervention is more likely to be effective when the family precedes the situation as a crisis. It's the counselor's role at this time to use the crisis to maximize the opportunity for positive changes. Remember that any crisis has full potential for danger and full opportunity.

The initial role of counseling is to:

1. Determine the nature of the crisis

2. Ask if there is a potential for harm or danger

3. Offer support and provide calming influence

4. Facilitate the exploration of options and help direct family to appropriate resources

13

The Goal in Crisis

∞

The goal in the crisis is to assess what has happen. When intervening in family domestic violence it is important to listen to each person's perception of the problem. The counselor wants to understand what the client /victim sees as the most important problem now. The victim may be sitting in your office or on your doorstep at midnight because she has been threatened with a gun and is afraid to go home. On the other hand, the highest priority may not be too disturbed the plans for her son's birthday party, schedule for the next day.

The counselor needs to solicit enough information in order to get an adequate assessment and appropriate plans can be established. Empathy and concern are important ingredients in this.

Whenever possible, it is helpful to obtain a history of previous violent episodes, along with a description of the stressors that have impacted the family. This will help to assess the potential for future violent episodes. A crisis situation may not allow for a detailed history, of course. The victim may be frightened and distraught and may not be a reliable source of information anyway. At some early point in the process, you need to get the necessary background.

When interviewing the family, it is important to be frank and honest with them. Ask specific questions about the violent incidents. If possible, talk with each one privately, as well as together, to get an idea of their interaction patterns. Learn what happened before, during, and after the episode.

Try to learn about the family background. Ask about each partners'personal and social history; the composition of the nuclear and extended family, and any violence that occurred in either partner's family of origin, any incident of the partners' being abused or neglected as children.

The information gathered will assist in assessing the family strengths and weaknesses. It should provide the counselor with an indication of how the extended family will respond to remedial actions such as separation. It will also help to identify stress points for the partner to use in coping with future situations.

One of the first priorities is to determine if medical attention is needed. If the injuries are severe and visible the need is obvious. Often battering does not leave highly visible evidence. Question the victim carefully and get her to a doctor if there is any possibility of injury.

Victims of domestic violence are often reluctant to use Medical Services for fear that this action will result in further violence. They worry about running up more financial obligations, causing their insurance coverage to stop, or that the abuse will become public. A mother may agree to medical assistance for the children but not for herself. Encourage a complete examination as soon as possible. Old injuries may never have been treated and maybe in need of medical attention.

Another important consideration in working with any kind of abuse is to file a police report. More and more states are establishing victim compensation programs for victims of domestic violence in violent crimes. These programs can provide financial support for living, medical and counseling expenses incurred as a result of being a victim of domestic violence or a violent crime. To get compensation, victims or their representatives must report the crime to law enforcement officers within 72 hours or as soon as reasonably possible (check the availability and specific requirements for your locality). After that, victims must apply within a specific period of time, usually one year, to the Victims Compensation Program to obtain benefits.

The crucial action at this stage of intervention is to report the incident to the police. If the woman waits too long, she may not be eligible for this source of help. Only recently have some states included victims of domestic violence among those eligible for benefits. For availability, find out what's available in the state in which the incident occurred.

Since victims of abuse experience a great deal of frustration, confusion, and pain, they require both emotional and physical support an award to make needed decisions. If you are the person to help a victim, you can help by being empathetic and sensitive to their needs. You should convey a willingness to stick by them throughout the crisis and should maintain and non-judgemental attitude. The goal at this time is to help facilitate decisions and not make permanent decisions for them. Emphasize the woman's responsibility to make decisions and take action. The abuse victim has learned to be helpless and needs to gain confidence and her ability to take control of the situation.

110

Fear is an important ingredient. The victim fears that the partner or spouse will retaliate with further violence. She may also fear court action or separation were result in the loss of a job for the abuser, loss of income, or loss of custody of the children. On the other hand, the abusive partner may fear the consequences of possible court action. This can become an opportunity for change in that the abuser may be amendable to outside help in order to avoid appearing in court and suffering the consequences of his actions. The children may fear separation from the family. It is importance of the counselor to do as much as possible to alleviate the fear but also be aware of its value in making changes.

As a facilitator, the counselor tries to assist the family members in making appropriate decisions and plans. An important part of this process is to help the family become aware of the pressure points in each of their lives that lead to violent episodes.

Another aspect of the facilitator's role is to assist family members in setting priorities for action. Victims of abuse have many factors to consider and may be overwhelmed by the complexity of the situation. A counselor or pastor can be a significant help in determining what steps need to be taken to alleviate problems in the family.

If the victim is a woman of faith, prayer should be a high priority component of that intervention process. First, prayer works to change things. All of the human interventions in the world may not change the mind of a battering partner or husband but God can. Prayer also has psychological value. Therein likely the victim has been praying in some fashion for relief from her abuse. Up to the crisis point, she may not believe her prayers have been answered. Prayer with another person tends to give renewed hope.

Be sure not to just pray and send the victim right back into the abusive situation. Pray with her but move onto practical forms of intervention that can be God's tools to change things for the better. Affirm the fact that God loves her. Emphasize God does not want her to suffer the abuse and she does not have to put up with that.

14

Options for Intervention

∞

If there is a high degree of risk, based on the abuser or victim profile, one or a combination of the following intervention strategies may be appropriate:

- Emergency shelter for the abuse victim and children

- Law enforcement involvement

- Court action

- Commitment of abuser to a psychiatric hospital

- Removal of children from the home

- Involvement of extended family, church, or community agencies in providing a place to stay and/or other necessities

Many pastors and counselors do not have training and experience in the casework aspect of intervention. If this is true, you may need to know how to make an appropriate referral. You need to know about existing services, the appropriate use of those services, key contact persons, emergency and regular referral procedures, and limitations of the resources (for example: waiting lists, eligibility requirements, cultural and language barriers, etc.), and along with regard to domestic violence.

In cases of domestic violence, the following services represent those that are most frequently needed. It is suggested that you make up a list with phone numbers and a contact person for the services in your community. You can start by looking up a directory for community services or by talking with other counselors.

- Child protective services
- Crisis intervention (24 hour availability on the phone or walk-in basis
- Police intervention
- Medical Care (emergency and ongoing)
- Child care
- Legal services for both partners protection
- Christian conciliation and mediation services
- Court services
- Alcohol/drug treatment (residential and outpatient)

- Financial assistance, such as aid to families with dependent children

- Victim compensation program (where available)

- Employment services (career counseling, job training and placement)

- Supportive counseling

- Mental Health Services

- Permanent housing

- Family planning

- Volunteer outreach

- Transportation

The concept of a shelter for victims of violence is important because it deals with one of the most difficult problems for victims of violence; that is where to go. Domestic violence usually takes place on weekends, in the late evening, or early morning hours when everything is closed. So many battered women spend hours on the streets, in a bathroom, locked in their cars or fleeing into the night without any personal items. Most of the victims have to return home and endure more violence or torment due to a lack of refuge.

One way of providing relief for battered women and their children has been the shelter or a safe house concept. The first safe house or refuge was opened in Chiswick, England in 1972. While there has been a variety of shelter models proposed, all of them meet the prime air purpose of protecting women and children from the abuser. Most shelters are located in a home like building, the address of which is not known to the community; this is for the safety purposes of the victim. Although the address is hidden from the community, the house is usually not. The point is not to encourage "hide and seek" type of game for batterers. Usually 20 women and children can be accommodated at any one time, depending on the facility.

There are a variety of philosophies represented in the operation of battered women shelters. Some have a very strong feminist orientation, others have a family perspective. You would be wise to visit several shelters in your area so you can become familiar before making referrals to the resource that matches the needs of the clients.

Why might it be better for woman to stay in a shelter, rather than with family and friends? A shelter can take the pressure off of the family who might otherwise be responsible for keeping the abuser at bay. Furthermore, shelters are accustomed to dealing with angry and upset husbands or boyfriends/partners, and have been fairly effective at keeping women and children safe. Shelters are only a temporary solution but can be very helpful in giving victims a protected place to sort out their feelings a consider options. Victims can also get comfort and feedback from women in similar circumstances. The staff of the shelters can also provide direction and resources for the victim in deciding what action to take next.

There are disadvantages to going into a shelter. The communal or group living situation is an abrupt change from the privacy of family living. The women will have to adapt to some rules, such as signing out, keeping curfews, keeping the location confidential. There are likely to be a variety of social, ethnic, racial and educational backgrounds represented, which can make the adjustment more difficult for some. Usually the maintenance, cooking and babysitting tasks must be shared by the women who live in a shelter. This may not be appreciated by some victims. Many shelters impose a rule that no physical form of punishment or discipline can be used with children. Some others find this very difficult and may be asked to leave if they cannot honor it. Despite the problems in adjusting to a group living environment, most women report the experience as being positive.

When a victim seeks intervention from law enforcement, there are two reasons why legal action might be helpful. First, if the victim is in danger, legal intervention may help keep the abuser from imposing further injury or trauma. Second, legal intervention may prove to be a way to get the family into long-term counseling and help. Although all self-referred counseling is theoretically preferable, in reality, court ordered treatment may be the only way some batterers will ever be helped.

When an assault has occurred, the first recourse is to call the police. In law enforcement, agencies use the call to intervene in a domestic disturbance because of its authority and 24 hour availability. Wife beating is a criminal offense in every legal jurisdiction of this country. Since spousal abuse is considered assault, it is against the law and the police could be called. But a counselor or pastor needs to know the limitations of law enforcement officers as well as their usefulness.

Think what would happen if all of the abused women did call the police! One expert reported some time ago that the number of these responses to minor family conflict exceeded the total number of murders, aggravated batteries, and all of the serious crimes. Studies have shown that only one out of five female victims ever call the police. At the same time, virtually every police department in the country is swamped with domestic disturbance calls. Seldom do the police resolve the violence problem to everyone's satisfaction. Most localities classified assault and battery as a misdemeanor. This often requires that the law enforcement officer must be a witness to this all before he or she can make an arrest. Often the violence has ceased before the law enforcement officer arrives. Also, the abuser may deny any violence has occurred.

In a detailed study of 380 cases of wife abuse, only 20 arrests of the men were made. Those arrests occurred only because the woman was visibly and seriously hurt, the man threatened the police, or the man became violent to the women in front of the officers. There is a tendency not to believe the victim and the bruises and accusations made by the victim are not usually sufficient to make an arrest. Arrests do make a difference.

For the abused woman or counselor wondering if the police can be of help, there are some general suggestions. Remember, the police don't want to get involved in domestic violence, and they are limited in what they can do when they arrive. Calling the police may not be a long-term solution unless it leads to the batterer getting help. If there is a high likelihood of danger, the police should definitely be called. They can provide temporary protection.

Unless the woman is willing to press assault charges against the man, there is

little the police can do unless you live in one of the few states with

mandatory arrest laws. They cannot make the man leave because it is his

home too. If the abuser is arrested, he will often be out of jail within a few

hours, angrier than before.

Legislation in a few states has tried to deal with domestic violence

by giving police mandatory arrest warrants for domestic disputes.

Overzealous or inconsistent application of this authority has resulted in both

the abuser and victim being taken off to jail, thus subjecting the victim to a

double peril. Not only is she abused, but she is taking off to jail because her

partner or husband says she hit him during the dispute.

Clarification of the mandatory arrest legislation has now been

implemented in states such as Washington to give law enforcement officers

better guidelines for their handling of a complaint. If there is evidence of

injury or the likelihood of injury, the officer will arrest the batterer. If the

batterer has left the scene, the police are obligated to search for a specified

period of time, such as 4 hours. Batterers cannot be released on their

personal recognizance. They must sign a no contact order which requires

that there be absolutely no contact with the victim for one year. This includes telephone, mail, third party or direct contact with the victim. The result is significantly more protecting for the victims. There are a limited number of states that has such legislation.

If the offender is very drunk and there is potential for injury but no obvious injury to anyone on the premises, the officer may make the determination to take the person to a detoxification unit rather than making an arrest. The officer will advise the victim of the right to file an assault or take other possible action in the office and may attempt to mediate a cooling off time. Sometimes the police are able to make referrals to community agencies, offer transportation to the magistrate's office to file for the assault or take to a safe place. In a situation when the victim has fled the home, the police may opt to notify the victim when the spouse or partner will be arrested so that she can return home and safely picked up the children and or her belongings.

Since only a few states have mandatory arrest laws, in the remaining states, the chances of the police taking action are better if the woman has obtained a peace bond or a temporary restraining order. A peace bond requires them to put up a certain amount of money which he forfeits if he breaks his peace with the person. Failure to post the bond can result in imprisonment. The peace bond may not be available in all states so you should check with someone familiar with the law in your area.

A temporary restraining order is a legal document issued by a judge and can be obtained without abuse being present, but may require some form of proof to show the possibility of abuse. It requires the abuser to stay away from the victim or to refrain from offensive conduct for a specific period of time. A restraining order is usually good for 10 days. After the initial 10-day period, the man has a right to contest the order. A hearing can be held to determine whether or not the order should be permanent. If the restraining order is violated, the violator can be cited for contempt of court which is a misdemeanor. Misdemeanor charges are generally resolved by probation or court ordered counseling. Short jail sentences are sometimes available. Civil remedies may also be available if a person is found in contempt of court.

The consequences of violating a temporary restraining order are often very slight and the victim certainly does not get much protection if the abuser has little respect for the law. Another problem is that, historically a restraining order could be issued only after a divorce suit has been filed; if a woman was not willing to file for divorce, formal protection was not available. Recent domestic violence laws have been altered in some states so that the dissolution procedure does not have to be initiated to issue a temporary restraining order.

Each state will be different, so you should check with a resource such as a domestic violence hotline and become aware of the procedures available in your area. Each state has its own definition and options for civil remedies, and you should become familiar with the regulations for service.

Another approach will be to use Christian Conciliation Services. Sponsored in many areas by the Christian legal society, this process is intended to be an alternative to the adversarial procedure found in most civil remedies. A conciliation service can recommend action in a dispute which can be implemented independently. They can make referrals to counseling and legal resources. Either informal or formal mediation procedures can be completed to facilitate agreements emphasizing mutual consideration and biblical principles.

The key ingredient is the requirement that both parties agree to a binding form of mediation. At the point of crisis intervention, getting both parties to agree on such a procedure will be most unlikely. The balance of power in most violent relationships, are heavily weighted toward the abuser. There is a possibility that the mediation process will end up focusing on what the victim does that displeases her mate, rather than giving attention to the fact the abuser is committing a crime and must stop. Most violent men need an authority figure, definite structure, and punitive consequences to direct them to change their behavior. Mediation may not be able to fulfill these functions, particularly during the crisis.

The counselor should have this information available, however, as it might be appropriate later in the process. Check your local area for the availability of conciliation for mediation services. The National Office of the Christian legal society can be contacted for referral assistance.

Unless an abuser is willing to enter a hospital for psychiatric treatment, then this option for help has limited possibilities. The involuntary commitment laws vary from state to state but do have some common procedures. The process begins when any concerned person makes a call to the involuntary commitment seen or the police. In the mental health unit it's called a "flying squadron", a number of mental health professionals may come to see the person in question. Their purpose is to make a determination of whether or not the abuser could be committed against his will. If there is a question of endangerment, the police may be involved and can take the person to a mental health facility where an evaluation is done.

The determination is based on whether another person is judged to be of higher danger to him-self or to others. The criteria; pretty stringent and almost requires the person to have a gun in his hand, pointing it at his victim.

If the team believes a person to be at risk to him or others, that person will be immediately taken to a mental health facility for observation. This usually lasts for 72 hours. And in that time; one of three things can happen: the person may be judged no longer a risk and released; the abuser may voluntarily agree to enter into treatment; a petition can be sought to commit the person for up to 14 days. If the person still meets the criteria for commitment after the two weeks, the formal legal process continues, possibly involving a jury trial which can result in commitment for at least six months.

Most involuntary commitments are terminated after the initial 72 hour period because most people cannot be shown, in that moment, to be dangerous to themselves or others. At any point they can voluntarily keep themselves in treatment but it may be difficult to maintain the criteria.

By the time most pastors or counselors become involved, the abuser is probably well into the remorse phase of the battering cycle. It would be unusual if the batterer could not exert enough self control to pass the

125

inspection of the involuntary commitment team. However, you should know the procedures in your area, should any present itself in a crisis situation.

Other options for violence-prone families may be receptive to services only doing the crisis phase. The pastor or counselor should first focus on helping the family in the immediate crisis. The pastor in a Christian family could have an advantage over secular professionals in helping bring about long-term effects. The violence family may have more of a commitment to a church relationship rather than an outside community agency. Once the crisis is past, the church still has an opportunity to be a caring community.

If families are unwilling to work toward long range treatment and goals, the counselor should not pressure them. Just make it clear that resources are available, should they want to use them. The counselor should always keep in mind the cyclical nature of domestic violence. It is probably going to happen again unless the basic methods of coping are changed. A pastor or the church's staff should contact the family on an ongoing basis as a natural part of the church's relationship with the family.

Be on alert for potential harm to the children after the crisis has passed. Some type of monitoring of the family may need to be done, in spite of their resistance. Usually, monitoring for the welfare of the children will be done by a community agency such as child protective services. It is wise for the pastor or counselor to establish a working relationship with several professionals and such agencies to ensure consistent an effective follow up.

Since situations of family violence are potentially volatile, they can present a substantial risk to anyone who becomes involved with the family. A counselor or pastor may be especially at risk when the abusive partner sees intervention as a threat to the status quo. National statistics indicate there are more police injuries incurred in responding to domestic violence calls than any other category.

For this reason; the pastor or counselor should take precautions to minimize personal risk, interview family members in a neutral setting. Don't get caught talking to a victim late at night in a place that could be considered suspicious to an abuser.

15

The Battered Woman
∞

Sheila sat nervously in the hospital waiting room, twisting her hair around her fingers. As the counselor came to greet her, she noticed an ace bandage wrapped around her wrist and bruises on her arms and face. While walking into the counselor's office, Sheila favored the left side of her body and winced noticeably when she sat down. When she was asked; why are you here, Sheila relayed a long list of horrible beatings and verbal abuse at the hands of her husband. Only after months of urging, with one of her close friends had she contacted a counselor. With great fear, Sheila scheduled the appointment with the counselor who had been recommended as a committed Christian who had helped many victims of violence.

Sheila expressed many emotions as she vacillated from anger to remorse. She knew she was right when she forced her husband to leave the home after beating her and threatening to kidnap the children. Her immediate concern was the order of protection hearing coming up. Sheila had been by told her attorney that she would have to testify in front of the judge and her husband about the details of her battering. She wasn't sure she could face it. The mother in law had called several times pleading to have the charges dropped. Her current concern was whether or not she should go ahead and seek the permanent order to keep her husband from returning home.

Counselors may work with many similar cases of abuse but most of them never cease to be amazed at the anguish caused when a victim of abuse makes the effort to extricate herself from an abusive situation.

The highest priority is to protect the victim. Using any combination of legal and social services, the victim and her children should be relieved of the threat of violence and abuse. Often safety is possible only by separating the couple. If the wife has gone to a safe house or shelter, the staff of that facility will play an important part in ensuring her safety.

The victim should make sure that she has a plan in place to escape to safety if her husband becomes violent again. It should include the manner of transportation, a place to stay, who to call for help, financial arrangements, and both short and long range plans for work or school. The husband should not know the specifics of the plan.

If the victim has filed assault charges or foreign order of protection or restraint, she will need a great deal of support. Many pressures can be applied to the victim that can leave her with strong ambivalent feelings about her decision. A counselor can be instrumental in giving support and encourage the victim to draw on her network of family and friends. Be alert to the possibility of the husband engaging in and strong lobbying efforts through that same network to get the wife to change her mind. All sorts of guilt can be induced by family members who have been duped by a remorseful husband. The sympathetic relatives may tell the victim that her abuser has changed his ways and that she should allow him to return home.

The next priority is to implement the combination of programs and resources that will lead to a determination of the violent behavior. Whether he acts voluntarily or by the order of the court, the abuser must get into a treatment program that will teach him other ways to deal with stress and conflict. Sometimes it takes a jail sentence to convince the batterer that his methods are not acceptable. Whatever the method; punitive or therapeutic, the goal is to stop the violence.

The final priority is in restoration of the relationship. Many pastors and counselors tend to move prematurely to some form of marriage counseling in domestic violence situations. This places the wife back in a destructive relationship before the behavior has had a chance to change, and it increases the likelihood that the cycle of violence will be repeated. Only when the abuser has made significant progress in controlling his violence, should a focus on counseling begin.

The woman, if married, has several options: she can return to the situation for no guarantee of changes, leave the relationship, return on the condition that the violence stops, or return only after being convinced the abuser/husband has learned alternative ways of behaving. Factors such as fear, economic dependency, and desire to save the relationship can weigh heavily on the woman's decision making. A counselor has the tough job of helping the woman maintain a sense of responsibility for her decisions. This is different because many battered women have trouble making decisions and taking appropriate action on their own behalf.

The most difficult aspect of counseling involves a battered woman's inclination to manipulate. The tendency to manipulate may subside when the stress level is low, but it is always there. As a result, the manipulation can be almost automatic. The woman can become frightened if the counselor offers to help. If the woman is still living with the batterer, she may be afraid that any changes in the relationship caused by the counseling can set off the abuser's anger. A counselor may view this wariness for reluctance to trust as paranoia. But it should be accepted as a natural outgrowth of living a life of terror. In order to be successful at manipulation, the woman always has to be on alert for ways to keep from setting off the abuser's anger. This can appear to be a frantic hysterical reaction, but makes since when relating to the victims goal of establishing a stress free environment for her abuser.

This distorted thinking; that she can always keep her abuser from getting angry or violent, must become a vital focus of her therapy. A counselor must realize that the woman has a very rare basis for her reluctance to make changes. The woman's fears must be taken seriously. This acceptance of understanding will help the woman relax and trust the counseling process. She may then be able to look at the reality of her beliefs, and eliminate some of her distorted assumptions. This will allow her to consider a less emotional and physically dangerous road map in achieving a balanced in her life.

Even after repeated episodes of violence, the victim will often minimize the situation after an immediate crisis has passed. The beaten and bruised victim may have come to the pastor requesting a place to hide from her ravaging abuser. A few days later, this same woman would turn around and intend to go home to an apparently remorseful abuser. The counselor may need to repeat discussions of previous attacks, having the victim include some of the violent details, to help convince or remind both the victim and the counselor of the dangers.

With these general features in mind, the counselor should help the woman explore options: if, when, and how should she go back to her abuser? This discussion should include how she would carry out her plan by drawing on her personal, family, a community of resources. When one has become very skilled at being helpless, deciding what to do and how to do it is not an easy task.

A battered woman has probably grown up with a low opinion of herself. In addition, her abuser has likely ridiculed and criticized her; leaving extreme doubts about her ability to function without him. One of the major goals of counseling the victimized woman is for her to grow to love herself in spite of her abusive history. This will occur slowly. Learning to love ourselves and learn to accept God's love is the foundation of a complete sense of being. If a woman has been a victim of domestic violence, helping her learn her sense of being and her purpose, will build self-esteem.

Most abuse women, particularly if they are Christians, wants their relationships to be successful. In spite of the pain they have experienced, they have sincere love and loyalty for their partner. When counseling these women, distinguishing between hope and the actions that help are important.

Hope has resulted from the cyclical nature of battering. The cycle has included periods of calm followed by escalating tensions, which leads to violence. After the violent episode, the abuser, much like many alcoholics, will promise to change. The victim clings to these promises of change. She wants things to be better. For a time, the abuser may become loving and kind. This behavior reinforces for the victim a hopeful attitude. The honeymoon is temporary, however, in most violent relationships; the tension begins to build again, leading to another episode of abuse.

There is nothing wrong with realistic hope, particularly hope built on God's promises. But the victim of violence needs encouragement and direction on how to avoid the trap of appeasement. Her hope is that she can keep her partner from getting angry and violent. A victim cannot control her abuser's feelings and methods of coping. The victim will need help learning to back off. Many abuse victims are rescuers. They take responsibility for the problems of their abuser, and the abusers are perfectly content with allowing their victim to take the blame. The end result is that the men are able to go about their lives without serious interruption. Neither do they have to experience many negative consequences for their behavior.

Battered women are often socially and emotionally isolated. A counselor or pastor should encourage efforts at re-establishing family and social connections. It is a process that should not be limited to individual counseling. The victim needs to be exposed to other women who have experienced similar traumas. These groups can be formed within a shelter or in conjunction with the counseling center or domestic violence agency.

If carefully formed and monitored, self-help groups might be established through the church. This could help meet the need for mutual support in sharing but with an added spiritual foundation. The church related groups should probably contain women who have had similar experiences. Do not place a battered woman in a bible study group where pressure will be placed on the victim to return to her abuser, forgive, or submit prematurely.

Several churches may combine personnel and conduct groups if there are not enough women from any one congregation to form a support group.

It might be advisable to try to bring the extended family together for several counseling sessions. Issues, such as continued safety procedures, channels of communication, how members may support the re-learning of habit patterns, and methods of support, could be discussed. It is likely that the victim learned some of her victim role from her parents.

If the victim experiences some pressure from her family or from his family, it might be good to draw them into some form of counseling activity. The victim will need support to stick by her decisions that may prove unpopular with her family; a counselor to direct contact with the family may help clarify the reasons for the victim's decisions.

Not all of the women's social contact should be heavy duty in nature. Encourage her to play and have some fun. Joining a bowling league or some other kind of active group and include some form of exercise is a good way of coping with stress, and it gives a victim the chance to make friends and find support.

Isolation, from the point of view of the victim, may be seen as abandonment. A victimized woman may have despair due to abandonment by her friends, family, pastor, an attorney. What about her own seclusion or

by the actions of others, the woman may feel that everyone has let her down.

Another aspect of isolation is ignorance of community resources. Be sure the

victim has phone numbers and descriptions of various social and legal

agencies. Resources should include: shelters, counseling services, abused

women's support groups, legal services for abuse women, sources for

protection orders, crisis phone lines, drug and alcohol treatment, sources for

financial assistance such as Social Security, welfare, or aid to dependent

children, churches, day care programs, career planning and placement

centers, and other agencies or programs that may exist in your community.

It is hard for a victim to re-introduce herself to society after isolation.

Don't rush the socialization process. The victim will be battling a great deal

of fear and hesitancy. She will need to be stretched in this area, but not

overextended. For the battered victim who experiences are filled with

legitimate fear and pain; it will take her inner thoughts to be changed to

produce a more productive mindset. The key to eliminating her worry is to

be able to place her trust in something solid, predictable, and helpful for her

growth.

16

Treating the Abuser

∞

Paul entered the group counseling room with an obvious chip on his shoulder. But standing 6 feet 5 inches tall and weighing in at about 250 pounds, who was going to argue with him? About one month earlier Paul had beaten his wife because he thought Brenda was having an affair with a friend of his. She denied any involvement, but Paul had lost control and Brenda ended up with 14 stitches and a broken arm. This had not been the first time this had happened, Brenda called the police and Paul had been arrested.

Only a few states have a mandatory arrest laws. Paul's state did, so he ended up having to post bail and signed an order preventing him from having any contact with Brenda until his case came to trial. Paul's attorney had told him; "the court would probably require him to complete a counseling program for men who batter". Paul reluctantly decided to check out a counseling center near his job even though he hadn't been sentence. It never hurts to make a good impression with the judge, his lawyer said.

As Paul slumped down into a chair at the edge of the room, he surveyed the rest of the "Wife Beaters" out of the corner of his eye. He thought to himself, they look like a bunch of jerks to me. Before Paul could ponder the situation much longer, a very ordinary man and woman entered the room and introduce themselves as doctors.

Most batterers do not seek any form of help, because they do not believe they need any. Any form of counseling that is received by the batterer is usually court ordered. Men who batter are also victims. They are victimized by their inability to channel their anger, lack of communication skills, fear of closeness, and their dependency on the women they abuse.

There are several assumptions or principles that underlie major forms of treatments.

1. Abusive anger is a learned behavior that stems of the basic nature of humankind. As Christians, we know that all humans have sinned according to scripture (Romans 3: 23). All of humanity is inclined to oppose God's plan. The form of the disobedience may change slightly from one generation to the

next but a constant fact of history is humanity's tendency to inflict pain on others.

Unless a person personally accepts God's work of grace, the patterns of violence and anger will continue. The abuser was moved to a point where he takes ownership and responsibility for his violent expressions. The abuser is solely responsible for his violence and abuse. No matter how many stressors there are, violence is never justified. Arguing can certainly be irritating, but no one is made to use violence. Choices are involved in violence, and each person must be held accountable for their choice. Most of all, the victim cannot cause or eliminate the violence of the abuser.

2. Abuse and hate starts in the heart of a person, but eventually the whole system is the defiled. Within a violent relationship, the abuser becomes more skilled at violence and the victim becomes more skilled at being a victim. This combination of events changes what the couple thinks, feels, and how they act. There are many parts in a relationship, but the uncontrolled anger must be stopped for the relationship to continue. The agenda becomes one of identifying the cues, prompts, or button pushing and events that lead to violence.

3. Outward action is a product of internal thoughts. Proverbs 23:7 tells us, for as he thinks in his heart, so he is. Abuse of anger is a function of how a person perceives the situation. For example, "she called me a dirty name". I can't let her get away with that; this will probably lead to some form of action to punish her. This monologue and its interpretation is the mechanism that can cause angry feelings and then to aggression.

4. Violence is motivated by low self-esteem and a sense of powerlessness. Both victims and batterers usually have histories of low self-esteem. This feeling of powerlessness often acts as a predisposing factor to violence. It's a vicious cycle. As a couple continues abusive interaction, the pain and frustration gets worse. This lack of effectiveness adds to their feelings of incompetency. These pessimistic feelings, in turn, create a more stressful, depressive atmosphere. The more negative the situation, now the more probable abuse becomes and intensity of the violence increases. Abusiveness is often an attempt to overcome personal feelings of powerlessness that lead to lowered self-image, guilt, and ones feelings of powerlessness.

5. Violence is likely when the couple does not have adequate problem solving or conflict resolution skills. Violence is used when a man doesn't know how else to solve a problem. It becomes essential for the couple to learn affective problem solving techniques for use in their relationship as well as with relationships outside of themselves.

6. The problems of the relationship should not be the initial focus of treatment. Counseling with the batterer present should not occur until the violence has stopped and the victim is no longer afraid. It's too dangerous to discuss the problems until everyone is safe. Any problems with conflict resolution and communication cannot be realistically discussed while the batterer is blatantly abusing power. Trust and confidence cannot be developed unless safety is achieved.

Most experts recommend a group format for working with men who are violent. Many treatment programs have emphasized separating spouses and providing separate group rehabilitation programs. Many of these programs have a strong bias towards helping the woman make a permanent break from the violent relationship. The emphasis on total separation may be based on the assumption that all battered women wish to end their relationships. The research shows most women do return to their partners. Many want counseling help for their batterers, who they still love. Most women seeking assistance for abuse would stay in the relationship if the violence could be eliminated.

Resistance and Denials

Almost all clients can be expected to show some initial resistance to treatment. Resistance should be considered a natural phenomenon. As such, it should be accepted by the counselor and not opposed. Some signs of resistance can simply be ignored. Some people just need to express their individuality, test the limits as they get on with compliance.

Sometimes a good way to approach resistance is to discuss it. Everybody probably has some initial reluctance to participating in treatment. Some of the sources of resistance might include:

1. Resentment. Since no one likes being told what to do without being convinced, the natural reaction is to dig in one's heels and resist.

2. Skepticism. Everyone tends to resist change. Change is unpredictable. It involves risk and uncertainty.

3. Pride. It's not easy for anyone to admit to making mistakes.

4. Embarrassment. It's difficult to talk about one's mistakes to others. There's also a tradition that a man's home is his castle; he shouldn't have to reveal to outsiders what goes on within his family.

5. Hopelessness. Many people have adjusted to frustration and uncontrollable circumstances by being apathetic, defeated and hopeless. This is very common in victims, along with the fear that their participation as a patient in discussion will be seen as a betrayal and lead to additional violence.

6. Anger. Sometimes people are mad about events occurring prior to the treatment program. They may be angry at the legal system, a mental health worker, or the police. Except the client's complaints and move ahead with the content of counseling rather than defend the sources of anger.

If the contents of the counseling process are positive and the abuser is treated with respect, the resistance would decline.

Generally, don't attack resistance head on or try to argue with the client.

Denial is a very common defense mechanism used by abusers. Men that batter, tend to minimize and deny their use of violence. The function of the denial is to avoid responsibility for the violent behavior in the need to change. Denial can also protect the abuser from depression and guilt that can come from a serious look at his situation. Denial can be observed in the following ways:

1. Blaming the victim. If he can blame her for the abuse, being she is the one who has changed.

2. Justifying his violence. The batterer would describe an incident, so the listener will conclude that his violent act was the only alternative. The focus will be on how good he is and how wrong the victim was.

3. Distorting and minimizing. The story will be accurate except that some facts will be changed to make him look good. If he broke her jaw, he will have only slapped her. If he was screaming insults for an hour, he only raised his voice a little.

4. Externalizes. He will place the reason for the abuse outside of himself. For example, he had a difficult day at work and was stressed out.

5. Omitting and lying. The story is not accurate because details are not told or fabrications are made.

The denial must be broken. This can be done by asking direct questions. When the blame is shifted elsewhere or there is an inconsistency, the counselor should point out the discrepancy or have the group comment. Often the group will do a better job than the leader in spotting lies and omissions.

The goal is to teach the batterer he is not in control of others, where he is always in control of himself. No one but himself can control his feelings, a motions, and thoughts. Breaking through the denial is to provide women information about the nature of the violence; how the abuser learned to be violent and how he uses violence to control others. The process begins by defining the four types of violence: physical, sexual, emotional /environmental, and social abuse.

Placing a time limit on treatment can be motivating to the participants. For most men the goal as an external motivator is to keep their relationships intact. To be lasting, the motivation must eventually move to a desire to change because they don't want the abuse to control their lives.

17

The Trauma View of Survivors

∞

If the abuser does not get the treatment necessary to assure the victim that violence will discontinue, she could potentially be looking at a future of responses that may cause her to respond like someone who has PTSD (Post Traumatic Stress Disorder). Abuse is a form of trauma.

Domestic violence is a form of trauma that can result in significant mental health distress for victims. Rates of clinical depression and post-traumatic stress disorder are higher among abused versus non-abused women, particularly if victims have experienced other lifetime trauma. While there are numerous interventions designed to reduce trauma-induced mental health symptoms, most were originally developed to address events that have occurred in the past (e.g., combat, childhood sexual abuse). Many domestic violence survivors are still under threat of ongoing abuse or stalking, which not only directly impacts their physical and psychological safety but impacts treatment options, as well. Little is known about the extent to which existing evidence-based trauma treatment modalities are applicable to, or require modification for survivors.

Domestic violence is a widespread and devastating phenomenon, with millions of women being assaulted by intimate partners and ex-partners across their lifespan. The ongoing pattern of coercive control maintained through physical, psychological, sexual, and/or economic abuse that varies in severity and chronicity. It is not surprising, then that; survivors' responses to this victimization would vary, as well. Some women can recover relatively quickly from domestic violence if it is shorter in duration and less severe and they have access to resources and support. Others, particularly those who experience more frequent or severe abuse, may develop symptoms that make daily functioning more difficult. Ongoing abuse and violence can induce feelings of shock, disbelief, confusion, terror, isolation, and despair, and can undermine a person's sense of self. These, in turn, can manifest as psychiatric symptoms (e.g., reliving the traumatic event, hyper-arousal, avoiding reminders of the trauma, depression, anxiety, and sleep disruption). Some trauma survivors experience one or more of these symptoms for a brief period of time, while others develop chronic post traumatic stress disorder (PTSD), a disorder that is a common response to overwhelming trauma and

150

that can persist for years. Survivors are also at risk for developing

depression, which has been found to significantly relate to the development

of PTSD. For those who have also experienced abuse in childhood and/or

other types of trauma (i.e., cumulative trauma), the risk for developing PTSD

is elevated.

Experiencing childhood trauma and/or severe longstanding abuse as

an adult can also disrupt one's ability to manage painful internal states (affect

regulation), leaving many survivors with coping mechanisms that incur

further harm (e.g., suicide attempts, substance use). Trusting others,

particularly those in care-giving roles, may be especially difficult.

While keeping in mind that victimization can lead to mental health

symptoms, it is also important to remember that for women who are currently

experiencing domestic violence, what may look like psychiatric

symptomatology (e.g., an "exaggerated" startle response on hearing a door

slam) may in fact be an appropriate response to ongoing danger.

Although wariness, lack of trust, or seemingly paranoid reactions

maybe manifestations of previous abuse, this "heightened sensitivity" may

also be a rational response that could protect a woman from further harm.

Similarly, a survivor's seemingly passive response to abuse can be

misinterpreted, as well.

While passivity might be a response to previous experiences of trauma, for survivors of domestic violence, it may be an intentional strategy used to avoid or minimize abuse that is beyond their control. Choosing to remain in an abusive relationship is often based on a strategic analysis of safety and risk. It is also influenced by culture, religion, and the hope (not always unfounded) that abusers can change.

Some domestic violence survivors turn to professionals for help with (PTSD) Post Traumatic Stress Disorder, depression, or anxiety symptoms that are interfering with their functioning and well-being. Trauma-focused treatments often include some form of either cognitive therapy or cognitive behavioral therapy and a great deal of evidence indicates that these approaches are effective across a variety of populations in reducing PTSD and depression.

However, these therapies are not effective for, desired by, or accessible to all trauma survivors; nor do they address many of the domains affected by longstanding inter-personal trauma. There are a number of issues that may influence how, where, and in what manner to provide trauma treatment to domestic violence survivors. For example, women still dealing with domestic violence are generally dealing with a myriad of pressing concerns (e.g., protecting their children, dealing with the legal system,

152

becoming financially more stable). They may have little time and insufficient funds for ongoing therapy sessions or completing homework outside of treatment. Low-income women in particular may have difficulty affording the needed childcare to attend therapy, and as a result of structural oppression, African Americans may have less access to insurance to pay for trauma treatment.

In addition, perpetrators of abuse may prevent women from seeking treatment or use their knowledge of their partner's treatment to continue their violence or threats. If the couple has children together, it is not uncommon for perpetrators to use women's help seeking against them, claiming that they are too "mentally ill" to effectively care for the children, which may discourage women from seeking treatment, as well.

Thus, a number of factors specific to experiencing domestic violence can impact both treatment accessibility and treatment outcomes. Clearly, more research is needed to test the effectiveness of trauma-focused mental health treatments for domestic violence survivors, especially if they are still being abused or are at risk for re-abuse.

In African American and Latino communities where survivors don't always have sufficient economic resources for treatment of their trauma; they are at risk for higher mental health outcomes, these groups have more signs of depressions, psychological distress and suicidal ideation.

There is hope for survivors of domestic violence. Although difficult and painful, recovery from abuse is possible. The healing process starts with recognizing how domestic violence impacts its survivors.

Survivors of domestic violence recount stories of put-downs, public humiliation, name-calling, mind games and manipulations by the abuser. Psychological scars left by emotional and verbal abuse are often more difficult to recover from than physical injuries. They often have lasting effects even after the relationship has ended. The survivor's self-esteem is trampled in the course of being told repeatedly that she is worthless, stupid, untrustworthy, ugly or despised.

It is common for an abuser to be extremely jealous and controlling, and insist that the victim not see friends or family members. The victim may be forbidden to work or leave the house without the abuser. If the victim is employed, she often loses her job due to the chaos created by such relationships.

This isolation increases the abuser's control over the victim and results in the victim losing any emotional, social or financial support from the outside world. This increases the victim's dependence upon the abuser, making it more difficult to leave the relationship. If she does leave, she often finds herself totally alone and unable to support herself and her children.

While normal responses to dangerous situations, fear and anxiety can become a permanent emotional state without professional help. Memories of the trauma can trigger intense anxiety and immobilize the survivor. Children may express their fears by becoming hyperactive, aggressive, develop phobias or revert to infantile behavior.

Because the trauma is so shocking and different from normal everyday experiences, the mind cannot rid itself of unwanted and intrusive thoughts and images. Nightmares are especially common in children.

Jitteriness, being easily startled or distracted, concentration problems, impatience and irritability are all common to being in a "heightened state of alert" and are part of one's survival instinct. Children's reactions tend to be expressed physically because they are less able to verbalize their feelings.

Survivors often blame themselves for allowing the abuse to occur and continue for as long as it did. Survivors feel guilty for allowing their children to be victimized. Sometimes others blame the survivors for allowing themselves to be victims. These emotions increase the survivor's negative self-image and distrustful view of the world.

Feelings of loss, sadness and hopelessness are signs of depression. Crying spells, social withdrawal and suicidal thoughts are common when grieving over the loss and disappointment of a disastrous relationship.

To recover from domestic violence, the survivor must:

- Stop blaming herself for what has happened and take responsibility for present and future choices.
- Stop isolating herself and reconnect with people in order to build a support network.
- Stop denying and minimizing feelings; she should learn how to understand and express herself with the help of a therapist.
- Stop identifying herself as a victim and take control of her life by joining a survivors' support group.

- Stop the cycle of abuse by getting herself and her children counseling to help heal psychological wounds and to learn healthy ways to function in the world.

Conclusion

∞

Domestic violence is not just an isolated incidence; it is an epidemic that reaches across all socioeconomic communities. From every community, there are women who will fall victim to domestic violence. They may not recognize that they are about to become a victim of something that is so traumatic in nature.

Women do not recognize that they are in an abusive relationship because often times they do not recognize the signs of abuse right away. The abuser is usually charming, very charismatic and loving in the beginning. Doing things such as; showering the woman with gifts, taking nice trips, enjoying fine dining and treating her extra special, winning over the family and friends with his charm until he has gotten himself into a position of power and control. An abuser may be pleasant and charming between periods of violence and is often seen as a "nice person" to others outside of the relationship.

It is important to note that domestic violence does not always manifest as physical abuse. Emotional and psychological abuse can often be just as extreme as physical violence. The lack of physical violence does not mean the abuser is any less dangerous to the victim nor does it mean the victim is any less trapped by the abuse. Additionally, domestic violence does not always end when the victim escapes the abuser, tries to terminate the relationship, and/or seeks help.

Women need to be educated on the causes and consequences of domestic violence and its traumatic affects. Attention needs to be given to ongoing efforts of safety, emotional skills development to address trauma related symptoms and long-term life goals.

A great deal more of research is required to understand domestic violence and how to respond most effectively to survivors. Most survivors have had multiple life trauma's (e.g childhood sexual abuse and/ cumulative trauma). Childhood trauma and or/ severe longstanding abuse as an adult can disrupts one's ability to manage painful internal stress, leaving many survivors with coping mechanisms that incur further harm (e.g., suicide attempts, substance abuse). Trusting others may be especially difficult. It is important to remember that for a woman who is currently experiencing domestic violence, may look like psychiatric symptomatology (e.g. "exaggerated startle response on hearing a door slam) may in fact be an appropriate response for ongoing danger.

We need to push for stronger laws that punish abusers and advocate for more treatment options for victims and abusers who seek help. Women don't always feel comfortable seeking help from law enforcement and surrendering to the treatment that police inflict sometimes when they are called on their abuser. Victims feel unsafe because of the feeling that the police may in turn harm them instead of help them. It is often times downplayed as just a harmless domestic dispute between intimate partners unless there is blood or bruises present.

Speaking out or seeking help often causes the victim to experience backlash from members of her community who believe that it is not good to air your dirty laundry for all to see and make herself and the family look bad. For this reason, many women stay in abusive relationships. This holds true more often for women in African American communities than any others.

161

As women, we need to believe that we are valuable, important and worth putting ourselves and our personal safety first. It is also important to find a therapy that works for you and examine ways to release the emotions you have because of your experience. In our society that might be the hardest thing of all.

It is my belief that a woman has a great opportunity for success at overcoming the emotional trauma of domestic violence and living a fulfilling life.

THE JOURNEY TO RECOVERY AFTER DOMESTIC VIOLENCE

∞

Recovery from domestic violence is a journey no one should take alone. The journey to victory is one day at time. It is important to have a support team of individuals along side of you to encourage you through the tough moments; when you feel like going back to the life you were familiar with and had become accustom to .

A victim's voice is important to healing; let's allow the conversation to begin. That same voice is also a way to raise consciousness about the profound effects of domestic/intimate partner violence.

Once a victim finds their voice, and a safe haven is needed; they can usually find refuge in a shelter or safe house if there aren't any options for safety with family or friends. If you or someone you know needs assistance, help can be found by calling *The National Domestic Violence Hotline* at:

(800) 799-SAFE (7233)

Notes

∞

[1] Ray Rice- CNN 9/15/2015

[2] Bradley, Jonathan. "Travis Browne accused of domestic violence after photos surfaced on Instagram." *Fox Sports*. July 9, 2019. http://www.foxsports.com/ufc/story/travis-browne-accused-of-domestic-violence-on-instagram-070915

[3] Silverman, Stephen M. "Josh Brolin Arrested for Spousal Battery". People.com. n.d. December 20, 2011. http://people.com/celebrity/josh-brolin-arrested-for-spousal-battery/

[4] Bill Clinton- Encyclopedia of World Biography, notablebiographies.com

[5] Brucculieri, Julia. "Halle Berry Opens Up About Experience With Domestic Abuse." Huffingtonpost. November 5, 2015 http://www.huffingtonpost.com

[6] "'Season 25 Episode 208'. *Larry King Live*. CNN, Atlanta. 4 November 2009. Television."

[7] The Business Insider, excerpt from "*The Song Machine: Inside The Hit Factory*", author John Seabrook 2009.

[8] ABC NEWS.go.com

[9] Biography.com

[10] Rubenstein, Janine, "My Sister's Unsolved Murder", *People Magazine*, April, 18, 2016, Web: people.com/tv/tamron-hall-says-sisters-unsolved-murder-still-affects-her-personal-life/

CPSIA information can be obtained
at www.ICGtesting.com
Printed in the USA
LVOW03s2200201217
560369LV00020B/2581/P